T0370436

THE
130
MOST
INTRIGUING
SONGS
THAT YOU
NEVER
HEARD

JEFFREY BRIAN ROMEO

authorHOUSE®

AuthorHouse™
1663 Liberty Drive
Bloomington, IN 47403
www.authorhouse.com
Phone: 833-262-8899

Published by AuthorHouse 03/27/2024

ISBN: 979-8-8230-2171-5 (sc)
ISBN: 979-8-8230-2172-2 (e)

Library of Congress Control Number: 2024902818

Print information available on the last page.

Any people depicted in stock imagery provided by Getty Images are
models, and such images are being used for illustrative purposes only.
Certain stock imagery © Getty Images.

This book is printed on acid-free paper.

Contents

Jeff Romeo's song lyrics elicit many emotions.....................xiii

40 Years 1
A Different Kind Of War 3
A Friend Indeed 5
A Wake-Up Story..7
A World Of Hate 9
Aint Got No Time 11
All American 13
All Of Damnation 15
Am I Dreaming.. 17
Angel Of Death.. 19
Attitude Of Death 20
Baby 22
Beauty And The Beach...23
Bibb County Line 25
Bite The Bullet 27
Borrowed Time 28
Broken Star...30
Cheers And Toasts 32
Cheers My Dear 33
Chip Away At The Rock...35
Country Music..37
Creatures Of Disney 39
Cut Me Loose 41

Dance With Me 42
Dead Man's Hand 43
Dead On Arrival 45
Den Of Thieves..46
Devil's Piano 47
Dine And Dash 48
Doctor Doctor 50
Dogs And Cats 51
Don't Cry...53
Drink And Drown 54
Even A Beast Needs A Goodnight Sleep.............55
Ever-last..56
Evil Ways 58
Famous For No Reason.......................................60
Feel Me Up 61
Fell Asleep 62
Finish What I Started 63
Girl Dad 64
Give Me Your Last Name.....................................66
Give Me Your Sympathy 67
God Of Chaos..68
God Paints The Skies..69
God Plays Centerfield 70
Going Insane 72
Graveyard Of Empires 74
Gym Rat 75
Happy Halloween...76
Head Over Heels 78
Hell, Aint A Bad Place...79
Hellenbach..81
Hide And Seek...83
Honey Bee...84
Huff And Puff 86
I know You're All Alone 88
I'll Drink To That...90

Imagine 91
It's All A Part Of Me 92
It's All Rock N Roll To Me 93
King Berserker 95
Let's Be Friends Forever 97
Life On The Road 99
Little Lady 101
Little Miss Understood 103
Living In A Small Town As God Smiled Down 104
Lucky Duck 106
Magic Carpet Ride 108
Man Made 110
March Your Feet 111
Medusa 113
Money Makes The World Go Round 115
Mother May I 117
Music 118
Never Enough 119
Never Touch Another Man's Hat 121
No One Will Miss Me 123
Not The First Time 125
One Drink, One Bet, And A Promise 127
One Hell Of A Night 129
One More Shot 131
One Trick Pony 133
Path Of Destruction 134
Perfect Mate 135
Pineapple Express 136
Ponytails And Butterflies 138
Popcorn And A Movie 140
Pot Of Gold 142
Promise Them Tomorrow 144
Ray Of Sunshine 146
Ring Around The Rosie 147
Romancing The Stone 148

Sad Prison Blues 149
Santa Is Real 151
Satisfaction Guaranteed 153
Scar Giver... 154
Scaredy Cat.. 155
Scratch And A Dent 157
She's a Diamond.. 158
She's Just Like Her Daddy.. 160
She Don't Know Defeat 162
Shred You Like A Doll 163
Single Mama.. 165
Something To Believe In 167
Stop, Listen, Learn, Start, Begin 169
Sunday Morning... 170
Sweet And Sassy.. 172
Sweet Emotion.. 174
Sweet Sixteen.. 176
Take Me Home Again 178
Take My Hand... 179
Take No Prisoners 180
Take Your Best Shot 182
Tell Me Something 183
Thank My Family and Friends (ride in the wind) 184
That's The Girl 186
The Circus 188
The Good, The Bad, And The Ugly 189
The One That Got Away 191
The Only Thing I Got To Do....................................... 192
The Pub (Celebration).. 193
The Real Me 194
The School Of Hard Knocks 196
The Secrets Of The Obscure....................................... 198
The Show Must Go On 199
The Way Life Goes 200
The Zone 201

Thee 203
There She Blows 204
This Heart Of Mine 206
Tiny Kisses On My Cheek 207
To The Moon 208
Tom The Turkey 210
Too Much Money 211
Vikings Always Return 213
Who Am I..214
Wicked Brew...215
Winter Is Coming 217
Wolf In Sheep's Clothing..................................219
Would You Leave This World............................220
You'll Be The Death Of Me 222

Jeff Romeo's song lyrics elicit many emotions

By Michele Gillis

Jeff Romeo's song lyrics will make you laugh, cry or maybe even cringe.

He had dabbled in writing over the years with poems and a few songs, but it wasn't until the pandemic hit that he really started churning out song lyrics and their diversity is intriguing.

So many songs in fact, that when he reached a 100 songs, he decided to publish them in book form. He worked with AuthorHouse publishing to create "The Best 100 Songs That You Never Heard".

He had each song copyrighted individually, but wanted to package them all together professionally in hopes that they could get noticed by someone in the music industry. He published his book in June of this year and it is available on Amazon or on his website.

"I would like to get someone's attention whether it is a musician, songwriter or publisher who says, 'He has some good stuff, let's check out his other stuff'," said Romeo. "Originally, my dream was to hear someone famous singing my song on the radio, just killing it and crushing it with my song. And somewhere in small print on the album, it reads co-written by Jeff Romeo. I want to be behind the scenes. I don't know what's going to happen."

The music he put to his songs is very basic, so he welcomes a musician taking his songs and turning them into something even better. Growing up, he was a fan of hard rock, heavy metal, classic and southern rock, alternative and country. So, his song lyrics are influenced by many different genres and could be paired with a variety of music.

His dream is that a famous musician would buy and record his songs one day.

"I know it would be Jeff's dream to have a well-known singer want to perform one of his songs," said Gary Lhotsky, Jeff's long-time friend. "I know Jeff loves Zakk Wylde. If Zakk Wylde did one of his songs, Jeff would be the happiest dude on Earth."

He didn't stop writing when he finished the book and currently has about 60 new songs and is churning out even more as you read this. He has been sharing several of his new songs on his Facebook page and his popularity has skyrocketed.

"I think my second round of songs are more dark and intriguing," said Romeo. "I have a wide range of musical interest that influences what I write."

Romeo will be the first to tell you that he has a very basic musical talent and can't really carry a tune, but that hasn't stopped him from creating songs that appeal to a very wide audience.

He taught himself a few key chords on the guitar and while he was home during the Pandemic he picked up his guitar and started strumming it and humming out words.

"The words seem to time out better when you do it with music," said Romeo. "That generated ideas in my head."

Musician Dave Hendershot of the Glass Camels feels Romeo has what it takes to be successful as a songwriter.

"I met Jeff in a pub a little over a year ago," said Hendershot. "He hadn't been published yet. He began to show me his work and published soon after. I think Jeff is a very creative and talented writer. He rhymes very naturally."

Lyrics can stir emotions inside of and help us to process and even celebrate monumental moments in our lives.

Romeo has always loved lyrics and felt that he could do as good or even a better job of writing lyrics as the musicians he listens to.

"I just started playing with the lyrics and making it my own story," said Romeo. "I felt like I was writing a movie. I can create anything I want in this song and make it work out whatever way I want such as happy, sad, scary, mean or sweet. I can make it do whatever I want. I love playing with words like with metaphors, idioms and certain phrases. I like twisting them around and making them your own."

When Romeo started writing songs, no one was more surprised than his sister.

"I thought he was just having some fun or maybe got bored and started a new hobby." said Jodi Muller, Romeo's sister. "I didn't think it would last long or go as far as it has. I mean I know he has always been deep into his music and had talent for drawing/art, but I had no idea he could write like this."

Muller said she thinks his songs are quite poetic, creative and well-written. Although, some she said she is not so fond of because she doesn't like the explicit songs.

A few titles that stood out from Romeo's postings and his book were Single Mama, Medusa, Honey Bee, Attitude of Death, Hellenbach, The Real Me, Dragons and Butterflies, Cruel World, Johnny Cash, Are we Dating the Same Guy?, Can't Always Get What I Want, Free Me and Busy Bee.

He feels his lyrics would go best with either country, rock or surf rock types of music.

"I try to be balanced," said Romeo. "I try to change up the subject matter to include things that people can relate to. Some of the songs are totally true and are about things that happened in my life. I got into a fight in college and ended up in a Christmas tree. That is in one of my songs. There is a lot of truth in there and some are sci-fi and far-fetched."

Lhotsky, who has known Romeo for 40 years, said Romeo writes what speaks to him in the moment and he loves the variety of moods.

"His songs can range from a darker side all the way to songs that are happy and sweet," said Lhotsky. "I think Jeff just found his calling in music, which is writing lyrics for songs. I just see his song writing as a way to marry a talent he has with his love for music."

Romeo said that not all of his song lyrics are about him or what he actually thinks.

"Some of it is what how I see how others live and I add theater," said Romeo. "Some truths, some partial truths and some total fiction. I'm ok with people guessing or thinking they know what it's about or if it's real or not, but it's not all just about me. As I said in book, maybe the fun part is trying to figure it out."

His sister, who knows him best, says she can see a parts of Romeo in the songs he writes.

"I think there's a mix of Jeff in the songs he writes," said Muller. "Some of it may be how his mind thinks, but not necessarily how he feels or lives. I mean, some of the songs are so out there that I pray they are only exaggerations of his imagination or things he interprets from outside sources. But some of the songs seem to really ring true about things he's done and how he feels."

Hendershot said that Romeo is very good at pushing the boundaries in his songs.

"Jeff has an ability to characterize," said Hendershot. "That is, come from his character's POV. I think he writes for him and that's the secret – no boundaries."

When Romeo started writing during the pandemic, he was sending his songs to his sister like crazy and she was amazed at his tenacity. It didn't surprise her at all that he reached 100 songs in no time.

"It's actually been kind of a joke that every time my phone 'pings' my husband says 'Jesus, is that another song?'" said Muller. "But, what's impressive is that he has written that many songs that really sound like artsy well-written poems. Some are better than others but I can see his growth as he keeps writing."

Muller said Romeo has always been very interested in music.

"I remember him to always be another level of smart when it came to the bands of the day," said Muller. "In high school, he knew everything about the songs and bands that played them. I can remember going with him to see Metallica. I think he caught the drumsticks at a Red Hot Chili Peppers' concert and he worshipped Guns N' Roses."

Muller said she is very proud of her brother. She said she hopes he sees this dream through, has fun trying and that it gives him fulfillment.

"He has tapped into a creative side of himself that no one knew he had, and he has put himself out there-really out there-like with posting on Facebook, singing his songs when he knows he doesn't sing very well," said Muller. "He stated his intentions from the start, which was to publish a book and to get his songs in the hands of other artists/musicians, etc. And I admit I thought all that sounded crazy at first, but he's doing it."

Lhotsky really admires Romeo for publishing his book.

"He puts his stuff out there and doesn't care what people think," said Lhotsky. "That takes some courage to put yourself out there. He is following his passion and I truly respect the hell out of him for doing that."

When asked what was a favorite song of Romeo's Lhotsky said "Zombie in My Bed."

"It's not in his book, but it was a metal song he wrote back in college," said Lhotsky. "I particularly loved it, but he will tell you it not that great. But he and I both loved heavy metal growing up so I think I am biased to that genre of music anyways and that made me really like Zombie in My Bed."

Hendershot is working with Jeff to put music to his lyrics to release a few songs in the upcoming months.

"I've been reading his work," said Hendershot. "When one grabs me, I write music for it. I come up with a melody line or a tag lick. We are currently in the composition phase. I go over and work with him a couple times a week. We've gotten together maybe four times and have 3-4 songs about ready for recording. I'd like to see an album come of his work. I'll be performing the songs in my solo shows. Ultimately, they will be for sale, rights and all."

Romeo would also like to make videos to go along with his songs, so stay tuned to his Facebook page and website for new developments.

He is single and has been a safety engineer with OSHA for 27 years. He has two children, Brooklyn and Tysen. Romeo grew up in West Virginia and moved to Jacksonville in 1997. He has a bachelor's degree in Safety Engineering from Fairmont State College and master's degree in Safety and Environmental Management from West Virginia University.

Romeo's book is for sale on Amazon.com and on his website, https://www.jeffromeosongs.com/. For more information visit his Facebook page, https://www.facebook.com/jeff.romeo.547

40 Years

My parents thought I would outgrow the music
scene
But now I can't seem to shake the leaves
They thought I would resent all my tattoos
And it was just a stage I was going thru

40 years later- Only one day smarter- Listening
to the same old songs
40 years later- I'm feeling much better- And I'm
right where I belong

I'm going to push my luck until my dreams
come true
I'm going to write more poems until I turn blue
I made some new friends that support my habit
Surrounding myself with others that have more talent

40 more years- Left on this planet- Time to make a difference
40 more years- Don't take it for granted- It's going to be
magnificent

I'm not afraid to make fun of myself at the end of the day
I'm not that serious and fun is the name of my game
If you smile once or twice or cry a tear or two
It means my words and music connected to you

40 years to go- I don't have a master- And I can stay out late
40 years to go- Life goes by faster- And I'm in quite a state

I filled my heads with rules, math and science
Worked hard in the industry of government and science
Made a penny or two and made plans to retire
But I'm too good looking and young to let myself expire

A Different Kind Of War

written 12/23

TV and news- AI and coups
Money and lies- Follow the clues

A different kind of war- Brews outside the walls
Fraud and deception- Tour of duty calls

Strategic moves- Twice removed
Kill them all- With no certain proof

A different kind of war- No one can trust
Words and information- Serene holocaust

China and Russia- Ukraine and Abdullah
Power and religion- Make strange bedfellows

A different kind of war- Robots and drones
Unmanned systems- An army of clones

4

A Friend Indeed

written 8/11/23

My buddies had too much to drink
So, they asked me to give them a ride
I was in the middle of playing my slots
And a little tied up at the time

Well, they thought they had a bright idea
So, they stumbled and fought for the keys
They drove the car thru the fairway
Avoiding the cops on the streets

Let this be a lesson to you and your friends
It could have been worse but ok in the end
Don't turn your back on those in need
Because a friend of mine is a friend indeed

Ed fell asleep in his own backseat
So, George woke him as they began to sink
They drove right thru the green
And landed in the pond of hole 17

Well, you can imagine the phone call to the pro
Yea, you got a car in one of your lakes
He's like one of our golf carts?
No, an automobile for God sake

Let this be a lesson to you and your friends
It could have been worse but ok in the end
Don't turn your back on those in need
Because a friend of mine is a friend indeed

Well, we look back and laugh at it now
It was one heck of a summer that year
We all have our little lessons in life
And crazy experiences to remember

A Wake-Up Story

If you could travel back in time and take one more shot at glory
Would you change your direction and write a different story
I'm not one to presume or to dwell on the past
But I can't help to imagine so I had to inquire and ask

How do you see yourself in a two-way mirror
What would you do with such capable power
Would you sit back, blend in and not say a word
Would you just stand by and watch as it all burned

If you could look and see into the imminent future
Would you save the world from mess and make it better
You may not be one to scheme a grander solution
But you may be able to offer a greater conclusion

Would you do what is right to protect the innocent
Without being selfish and empowering the dominant
Would you fly to the moon and reach for the stars
Would you make like a rocket and launch up to Mars

It would be interesting to know how you would pave your way
I hope this was an amusing way for you to wake up and start
your day

A World Of Hate

written 7/18/23

I got a million pieces lying under
my bed
Biting fingers off the hand of fate
That makes dinner for the three
of us
Rubbing shoulders with the devil's
guest

The creeps are creeping in the
dead of night
The hair is standing on my neck and back
My eyeballs are getting bloodshot again
Everything itches likes snakes under my skin

I may look like a loser, but no one forgets my face
Tenderizing souls for the dead, living in a world of hate
I may look like no other, but I will deliver your fate
Tenderizing souls for the dead, living in a world of hate

Your body parts are so perfect
I can taste them like bread and wine
The smell of lost souls intrigues me
So, I grab and suck just like a leach

I can't just leave you hanging about
My neighbors with think I'm a freak
The hounds in the closet will want to bark
When they chew and devour the leftover parts

I may look like a loser, but no one forgets my face
Tenderizing souls for the dead, living in a world of hate
I may look like no other, but I will deliver your fate
Tenderizing souls for the dead, living in a world of hate

Aint Got No Time

written 9-3-23

She left me hot and bothered when I ran out of dollars
So, I grabbed her by the p***y, time to call my lawyers
She stung me like a bee right between my knees
I swelled up like the tropics but that's alright with me

Aint got no time to complain, it's time to disengage
Aint got no time to explain, I got to catch my plane
Aint got no time for funny games, it's time to rearrange
Aint got no time to campaign, I got to catch my train

I began with good intentions but then I got no more attention
I ate her low hanging fruit then her tree gave me lemons
I promised her the world, two dogs, a cat and a bird
Then she fell off a cliff, yea she got what she deserved

Aint got no time to complain, it's time to disengage
Aint got no time to explain, I got to catch my plane
Aint got no time for funny games, it's time to rearrange
Aint got no time to campaign, I got to catch my train

All American

[Dedicated to Captain Crunch]

I used to be an All Star, but I'd rather be known as a father, son and a dear brother
I used to drive a fast car, but I'm better known as a husband, friend, and a Pittsburgh Steeler

If you thought you knew me, you wanted to fight me
But if you really knew me, you wanted to be me

I'm just a hard-headed, red blooded, All American that will miss my family and friends
I'm just a quick witted, full blooded, Bridgeport Indian that was brave until the very end

My dog's name was Speedy, and I used to dress up like Ace
Frehley
My friends are going to miss me because I used to be the life
of the party

When you think about me, you will cry for me
But when you really think about me, you will smile for me

I'm just a hard-headed, red blooded, All American that will miss
my family and friends
I'm just a quick witted, full blooded, Bridgeport Indian that was
brave until the very end

(Anthony will always be an All-American legendary friend)

All Of Damnation

written 7/13/23

The night fall lays her blanket on the children of the forest
The wind blows out the candles, cast her shadow on the canyons

The beauty of the mountains illustrates like water fountains
The sun shines like a diamond, brings warmth to the island

Under God and nation, she pledges her allegiance
Under all of damnation, our fate will await us
Intentionally courageous, her smile is contagious
Under all of damnation, eternity will await us

She has the soul of a child that gently calms a storm
A rainbow for the skyline and a flower with a thorn

A mother like an Angel that feeds you late at night
Another rare encounter to fill you with delight

Under God and nation, she pledges her allegiance
Under all of damnation, our fate will await us
Intentionally courageous, her smile is contagious
Under all of damnation, eternity will await us

Am I Dreaming

written 1/24

Outside my window, I saw a thousand tiny people
They held me down and then they tied me up spread eagle

I broke loose and I escaped on a flying unicorn
Hunted by a dragon thru a raging fire storm

I hid inside a secret room that turned into a cave
Chased by a giant eyeball thru a life-sized corn maze

Fascinating, vivid, and lucid- Some are nonsense, and some
are stupid

Am I dreaming or am I awake
Is it real or is it fake
Often lost but never found
Lies and truth area all around

Godzilla and T-Rex took over my city
Aliens from outer space tried to seduce me

Sometimes I can't even find the bathroom door
Other times I'm naked at the grocery store

Too much coffee and too much caffeine
I keep on falling down and losing my teeth

Persistent, graphic, and epic- Some have meaning and some
are evocative

Am I dreaming or am I awake
Is it real or is it fake
Often lost but never found
Lies and truth area all around

Some are happy and some are sad, some are good, and some
are bad
When I forget them, it makes me mad, so I write them down
on my scratchpad

Angel Of Death

An Angel with no wings stole my heart and my soul
Neglected my feelings and let me shiver in the cold
I pouted and I shouted, and I cried to Kingdom Come
Lethargic and apathetic, I'm feeling vacant and numb

Angel of death with cheap parlor tricks
An acquired taste rolled right off her lips

The eyes of an Angel and soft skin like a baby
Too smart for her own good with a kiss proven deadly
Intoxicated with love as I begged for more wine
Privileged and sophisticated, she's polished with shine

Angel of death with cheap parlor tricks
Precious cargo with deep inner conflict

Attitude Of Death

written 9-3-23

I took an arrow thru the heart
And a knife in my back
A bullet to the head
And an air raid attack

I took my final breath
As I lit my cigarette
Smoke filled my lungs
I have an attitude of death

Attitude of death- don't care what happens next
Attitude of death- there aint no coming back

I was left behind for dead
In the jungle of the East
Laid there and I died
All alone in the weeds

I took one to the chest
Suffered cardiac arrest
My veins bleed red and blue
I have an attitude of death

Attitude of death- don't care what happens next
Attitude of death- there aint no coming back

I'm nowhere but I'm free
Drifting a million miles
The stars and Angels sing
Come to me my child

My battles laid to rest
And my life was second best
Sold my soul for my country
I have an attitude of death

Attitude of death- don't care what happens next
Attitude of death- there aint no coming back

I took an oath on the whim
And went to war when I was young
I sacrificed my future
And my youth when I was done

Baby

written 1/24

My baby wants to fall in love
My baby wants to kiss and hug
My baby wants to make romance
My baby wants to sing and dance

Baby, baby when you dress with style
You get me feeling kinda wild
Baby, baby my honey child
You make my face a giant smile

My baby wants to hold my hand
My baby wants to see a band
My baby wants to wear high heels
My baby wants a fancy meal

Baby, baby when you dress with style
You get me feeling kinda wild
Baby, baby my honey child
You make my face a giant smile

Beauty And The Beach

written 8/3/23

The coast is clear for a walk in the park
I don't make waves or stay past dark

Blue skies, sunshine
Cool breeze, I'm feeling fine
Suntans, seashells
High tides, and top sails

Skateboards, bike rides
Fireworks on the 4th of July
Swimsuits, sandy cheeks
Natural beauty, and the beach

The sea is calm for a skinny dip
I don't rock the boat or abandon ship

Cold drinks can't get enough
Palm trees and coconuts
Meet me at the sandbar
The beers on ice and free of charge

Sun burns where the sun don't shine
Big Kahunas and no tan lines
Swimsuits and sandy cheeks
Natural beauty, and the beach

Bibb County Line

written 7/18/23

I went down the wrong way
on a one-way street
They locked my up in prison
just like a piece of meat
I didn't know she was the
wife of the Deputy
My ego and mouth will be
the death of me

The town knows something but they aint complaining
The storm is brewing, and the south is burning
Don't stop for shopping or spend your time
Don't stop for nothing at the Bibb County line

My life is getting mixed up just like a maze
Lost my train of thought, let me count the ways
Don't stop for shopping or spend your time
Don't stop for nothing at the Bibb County line

My phone lost all connection just North of Perry
The devil called me darling just West of Shelby
I left my truck for just a minute on the side of the road
Searching for a rainbow and a pot of gold

The town knows something but they aint saying
The storm is brewing, and the south is burning
Don't stop for shopping or spend your time
Don't stop for nothing at the Bibb County line

My life is getting mixed up just like a maze
Lost my train of thought, let me count the ways
Don't stop for shopping or spend your time
Don't stop for nothing at the Bibb County line

Bite The Bullet

written 7/13/23

Got no time for prison- I only got a minute
Got to keep on moving- Buy my one-way ticket
I'm sinking in my bed- Sleeping with one eye
Waiting for the moment- Tell my cell goodbye

Hold it down and push it
Pull it out and slide it
It may not be perfect
Got to bite the bullet

Working on the chain gang- Or cooking in the kitchen
Need to get lined up- Got to assume the position
Looking out my window- I got all day and night
Freedom's just a pipe dream- Got to tease my mind

Hold it down and push it
Pull it out and slide it
It may not be perfect
Got to bite the bullet

Borrowed Time

Every day we live on this planet, there are many hazards that we face
Life is nothing more than a miracle, we must maneuver with style and grace
It's like playing chess with checkers or cards with the neighbor kids
Sometimes you just get lucky and sometimes you get annoyed and sick

Some of us see it coming and some of us have no clue
Some of us think we are winning but in the end we all lose

Living on borrowed time from the day we were born
Living like there's no tomorrow until the day we're gone

Every night as we pray when we lay down and go to bed
We must thank God for tomorrow and for waking us up again
It's like we are living on borrowed time and a swindler is holding the clock
You can turn on the lights and candles, but midnight is coming for all of us

Some of us see it coming and some of us have no clue
Some of us think we are winning but in the end we all lose

Living on borrowed time from the day we were born
Living like there's no tomorrow until the day we're gone

Broken Star

written 7/24/23

It was nice to know you from the time we were kids
Even after we grew up, we still remained friends
Haven't seen you forever but I remember our youth
I remember the good times and the way you were cool

Hello to goodbye in less than a life
Hello to goodbye in the time that has died
Goodbye my good friend, you played a dear part
Say hello to heaven now that you're a broken star

A family of wolves is always a pack
A brother, a son, you made an impact
You broke all the records from our small home town
You taught all the cubs how to become a hound

Hello to goodbye in less than a life
Hello to goodbye in the time that has died

(dedicated to Matt)

Goodbye my good friend you played a dear part
Say hello to heaven now that you're a broken star

Teachers hated to say they loved you
But we all know you loved them too
One of the tough ones but you still had a heart
Thank God for your looks cuz you weren't that smart 😊

Cheers And Toasts

written 12/23

Hope the new year brings you happiness and wealth beyond your years
I hope it opens the windows and doors to what you've been looking for

Cheers to a clean slate that takes you back to the start and to a better place
Cheers to a new year and another chance to erase the past and create romance

Hope the new year brings your dreams to fruition and your straw to gold
I hope you meet the new challenges, and you accomplish your goals

Toasts to good health, prosperity, and a fortunate life
Toasts to my family and friends and to all a good night

Cheers My Dear

written 8/9/23

All I really want to do is run away with you
Pack us up some food and some bottles of brew
Quick trips home and a few good shows
Grab my clothes and hit the road

Life is a little less complicated when we get a little bit intoxicated
Life is a little more adventurous when we get a little bit more generous

Cheers my dear, touch the glass
Sip and stir, down the hatch
Cheers my dear, tip the cup
Feel my bump, bottoms up

Last night I spent the day trying to obey
Drinking my way at the local café
I got all lit up with a 10 cent cup
Telling that chump not to interrupt

Life is a little less complicated when we get a little bit intoxicated
Life is a little more adventurous when we get a little bit more generous

Cheers my dear, touch the glass
Sip and stir, down the hatch
Cheers my dear, tip the cup
Feel my bump, bottoms up

Chip Away At The Rock

written Oct 11

Well, they dig that dirt all day- And they come home late at night
They make no bones about it- Wake up before the light
Well, they don't take sick days off- And they eat lunch in the dark
They call it as they see it- Chip away at the rock

Chip away at the rock- Working around the clock
Pay my dues to the local- Learn to work before I walk
No time for family time- No cookouts at the park
Sweat because they love it- Chip away at the rock

Chip away at the rock- Chip away at the rock
No break until they make it- Chip away at the rock

Well, they breathe in shit all day- And the boss mans never pleased
He screams his lungs out loud- It's 110 degrees
Well, they turn that timesheet in- And the tax man takes his cut
They give it back to Sam- Chip away at the rock

Chip away at the rock- Working around the clock
Pay my dues to the local- Learn to work before I walk
No time for family time- No cookouts at the park
Sweat because they love it- Chip away at the rock

Chip away at the rock- Chip away at the rock
No break until they make it- Chip away at the rock

Country Music

written 8/27/23

Hear that train coming thru my head
Time to get up and get the chickens fed
Been chopping firewood since the day I was born
Mining my business and planting corn

I'm on a country western music kick- Riding horses and raising pigs
I got country music in my veins- I thank God when it rains

I'm in a country western music band- Blood and calluses on my hands
I got country music on my mind- Sing I'm so lonesome when I cry

Milking black cows in the bay of the barn
Square dancing music down on the farm
Making ends meet can be a strain
Working hard in a house of pain

I'm on a country western music kick- Riding horses and raising pigs
I got country music in my veins- I thank God when it rains

I'm in a country western music band- Blood and calluses on my hands
I got country music on my mind- Sing I'm so lonesome when I cry

Up at the crack of dawn since I was 5 years old
Don't matter if the sun shines down, hot or cold

Creatures Of Disney

written 8/6/23

Mickey was a mouse that kissed ass for cash
Donald was a duck that sold dope and quack
Minnie was a slut that danced on a pole
Goofy was a dog that was doing blow
Tigger was a cat that earned his stripes in jail
Winnie was a bear that didn't exhale

They may sing, dance, be merry and gay
But they also drink, snort, fuck and play
They may look cute, fun, jolly and sweet
But the creatures of Disney are sleazy and cheap

Genie was a junkie that drank from the bottle
Buzz was a toy that spend time at the brothel
Sleepy was a dwarf that slept all around
Rapunzel was the blonde that always went down
Peter was a fairy that flew high as a kite
Daisy was whore that smoked a crack pipe

They may sing, dance, be merry and gay
But they also drink, snort, fuck and play
They may look cute, fun, jolly and sweet
But the creatures of Disney are sleazy and cheap

Snow White was a bitch that banged her way to the top
Woody was a cowboy with a huge giant c**k
Lady was a tramp on the corner doing tricks
Chip and Dale were brothers that were total dicks

Cut Me Loose

written 12/23

These streets will eat you up for breakfast then spit you out to waste
Steal your pride, joy and necklace, and leave you alone in disgrace

No time to die- Hang em high
If you cut me loose- I'll drift and fly
Cut me loose- From the noose
Wash my hands- And clean my boots

These snakes will nickel and dime you to death then shake you upside down
Steal away your last breath and leave you 6 feet underground

No time to cry- Touch the sky
If you cut me loose- I'll run and hide
Cut me loose- From the noose
Wash my hands- And clean my boots

The rats in the maze will figure it out if the get hungry enough
Swim, or starve and drown, run to the hills and pack up their stuff

Dance With Me

written 8/26/23

I'm so hungry for life I could eat a horse
I've lived 5 lifetimes without any remorse
I've been around this world many, many times
Danced in London, Paris France, and Hammerstein

Dance with me and
play my tune
Drink some tea in
the afternoon
Dance with me and
hum my song
Drag your heels all
night long

I'm too rich to be lonely so I buy my happiness
I crashed my train without any consequence
I've been knocked down again and again
Picked back up, kicked, bite and got revenge

Dance with me and play my tune
Drink some tea in the afternoon
Dance with me and hum my song
Drag your heels all night long

Dead Man's Hand

written 11/21/23

When you're a minute from the truth and death comes knocking on the door
You start to realize that you were dying from the day you were born
When you start to hear the music and the funeral bells ring
You better smoke em if you got em when the fat lady sings

Not even a magician can hold his breath when the hourglass runs out of sand
Not even a gambler can cheat death when he plays with a dead man's hand
Play your cards the way they land- You can't beat God with a dead man's hand

When you're in the wrong place at the wrong time and the clock strikes midnight
You start to realize that you were dead wrong and stare at the light
When you draw the shortest straw and fall on the sword
You better pay your debts and pray to the lord

Not even a magician can hold his breath when the hourglass runs out of sand

Not even a gambler can cheat death when he plays with a dead man's hand

Play your cards the way they land- You can't beat death with a dead man's hand

Dead On Arrival

written 11/30/23

Laying in my bed with the sheets overhead
Fever turns to chills and my body sweats
I'm here all alone just me and my phone
Nobody calls me to find my bones

I'm dead-on arrival- No air in my lungs
Dog ate my heart- And cat stole my tongue
I'm dead-on arrival- No signs of life
Find the clues- And solve the crime

Blood, sweat and tears but nobody cares
If you fade away or if you disappear
I buried your head behind the shed
Nothing is real and it's just pretend

I'm dead-on arrival- No air in my lungs
Dog ate my heart- And cat stole my tongue
I'm dead-on arrival- No signs of life
Find the clues- And solve the crime

Den Of Thieves

Not quite what I expected in this quiet little joint
It was ripe for the taking, so I got right to the point
I covered up my face and pulled out my piece
Handed her a note and said get on your knees

I got high class dreams and I'm full of schemes
Living like a fox in a den of thieves
I'm a mean machine, make you beg and scream
Living like a wolf in a den of thieves

Found a quaint little home all alone in the burbs
Took my sweet ol time as I went thru her drawers
I'm mean as a bear and as cold as a snake
Have a grip like a crab that you can't escape

I got high class dreams and I'm full of schemes
Living like a fox in a den of thieves
I'm a mean machine, make you beg and scream
Living like a wolf in a den of thieves

Devil's Piano

No plans past today- The wishes waste away
In between the trenches- There are no more fences
Woken by the thunder- And the sound of machine gun fire
Welcome to no man's land- Where I make my final stand

The bastards shoot their ammo
The graves are cold and shallow
The trumpets start to fade
And the devil plays piano

It feels like Christmas Eve- The quiet echoes grieve
A momentary pause- To recoup the fallen ones
The front lines force you in- It's a chilling way to end
Welcome to no man's land- Filled with blood, dirt and sand

Muddy, flat, and narrow
The land is dust and fallow
The war drums start to beat
And the devil plays piano

Dine And Dash

written 8/16/23

Sit right back- Eat your meal
Tip your hat- You know the deal
Take a bite- Have a drink
Talk is cheap- No time to think
Set the pace- Don't be last
Run don't walk- I'm super-fast

Rack my brain- Got no cash
Fail to pay- Dine and dash
Empty tank- Got no gas
Drawing blanks- Dine and dash

Grab the keys- Out the door
Hit the road- You know the score
The chase is on- The catch is bad
I'm on the run- Don't look back
One more time- Back for more
Fill me up- At the store

Rack my brain- Got no cash
Fail to pay- Dine and dash
Empty tank- Got no gas
Drawing blanks- Dine and dash

Doctor Doctor

Laying sick in bed, tucked under the covers
Can't control the temperature as it gets hot and colder
A throbbing in my head and the lights hurt my eyes
My sheets are full of sweat but my dog is by my side

Doctor, doctor help me please
Help me cure my lame disease
Doctor, doctor help me please
I'm all out of antibodies

I can't go to work and my hot skin burns
My house is contagious, full of bacteria and germs
I just want someone to make me some soup
Carry me to the couch and turn on some hoops

Doctor, doctor help me please
Help me cure my lame disease
Doctor, doctor help me please
I'm all out of antibodies

Dogs And Cats

written 7/15/23

Dogs and cats are like brothers and sisters
They may scratch and bite
But in the end
They're always there for each other

Dogs and cats make you feel loved and special
Like a parent they help you grow
But unlike people
They're never superficial

Dogs and cats living together
As they play, chase, and obey
Although cats may rule the world
Every dog will have his day

Dogs and cats living together
As they eat, sleep, and urinate
Although cats may rule the world
Every dog will have his day

Dogs and cats are curious by nature
Clumsy, kind, and loyal
But just like my kids
I still don't know which one is smarter

Dogs and cats are great companions
By your side until the end
But they will test your patients
And your intuition

Dogs and cats living together
As they play, chase, and obey
Although cats may rule the world
Every dog will have his day

Dogs and cats living together
As they eat, sleep, and urinate
Although cats may rule the world
Every dog will have his day

Don't Cry

With the wind at my back and my troubles behind
It's time to set sail and keep toeing the line
Like a breath of fresh air in the still of the night
I'm guided by stars and the soft moon light

Blow me a kiss and tell me goodbye
I'll see you again so please don't cry

Please don't cry for me mama
Please don't cry for me

I packed up my bags and I drifted away
I left you alone with news from yesterday
My ship got lost as it rocked and it swayed
Like a sunken treasure on my final crusade

Spread my wings it's time for me to fly
I'll see you again on the other side

Please don't cry for me mama
Please don't cry for me

Drink And Drown

written 8/3/23

There was once a time,
when I was young and blind
I could love you twice and
make you lose your mind
I'm a two-time hand me
down, a thief, a prince, and
rodeo clown
Get on board with me, you
know I get around

Hammerhead's and Bunny's, got no time to study
It's Thursday drink and drown, got to wear my Crown
Valley Falls and Arden, got to earn my pardon
Bearded Clams and Yann's, got to eat it like a man

Many, many years ago, when I was high on a plateau
I could go all night and leave before you know
Dancing shadows of the night, thunder, lightning in the sky
It's a perfect storm, watching the world go by

Hammerhead's and Bunny's, got no time to study
Thursday drink and drown, got to wear my Crown
Valley Falls and Arden, got to earn my pardon
Bearded Clams and Yann's, got to eat it like a man

Even A Beast Needs
A Goodnight Sleep

written 1-24

I'm a mean alligator- I'm a croc on the Nile
When the sun comes up- I get hungry and wild
I'm a dog on the loose- I'm a wolf on the prowl
When the full moon rises- You can hear me howl

When the wind screams loud like a
chant from a crowd
It helps me sleep with a hypnotic sound

I'll be dreaming of feast and all I can eat
cuz even a beast needs a goodnight
sleep

I'm a man without a heart- I'm a cowardly lion
When the sky turns black- There's a storm on the horizon
I'm a beast of a burden- I'm a wreck of a soul
When the ground starts to shake- I lose all my control

When the wind screams loud like a chant from a crowd
It helps me sleep with such a peaceful sound

I'll be dreaming of feast and all I can eat
Cuz even a beast needs a goodnight sleep

Ever-last

written 7/24/23

Well, I knew right from the start
She had a kind, modest heart
An accent from down south
Classy, sexy and smart

She has stage presence and style
Bright blue eyes that make me smile
She has my back when I'm not around
And by my side when I'm feeling wild

We walk this path together on the road to happiness
Our love will last forever and the journey ever-last
We will keep on learning about the rules of life
Our love will keep on burning and the journey ever-last

Well, I knew right when I saw her
She had a cute nervous manner
She looked so proper and pretty
As we shared our first dinner

She's a precious diamond in the sky
With Angel wings flying high
She wears her auburn hair just like a queen
Pale skin, red lips as pretty as I seen

We walk this path together on the road to happiness
Our love will last forever and the journey ever-last
We will keep on learning about the rules of life
Our love will keep on burning and the journey ever-last

Evil Ways

written 7/25/23

The curse of the evil dead is under the shadow of my evil ways
For I know the evil that you do
Because I am the governor of fake truth

I bleed in your evil veins when you dine on my guilt and fear
For I know the evil that you stole
Because you wrote your name on my soul

The past, present, and future will be buried in a deep grave
To hide the pain and the evil of your ways
The terrible beast must hang from the gallows like a slave
Let me count the days and the evil of my ways

58

The curse of the evil wretch rise from the ashes of my evil ways
For I know the evil that you speak
Because I am the darkness that you seek

I see the evil in your eyes when you look at your next meal
For I know the evil that you created
Because your ego made you say it

The past, present, and future will be buried in a deep grave
To hide the pain and the evil of your ways
The terrible beast must hang from the gallows like a slave
Let me count the days and the evil of my ways

Famous For No Reason

written 7/14/23

Ben was a just an Army General, but he had a secret gift
John was just an average Joe, but he got cut off at the tip
Robben was just a lonely island, but the prison was up to no good
George was just a good neighbor, but he shot before he looked

Infamy and notoriety, power, money, and celebrities
If it wasn't for the treason, they'd be famous for no reason

Kato was just a burn out, but he looked like a movie star
Mona was just a pretty face, but was a stolen piece of art
Aaron was just a player, but he out punted his coverage
Stephen was just a waiter, but he had brothers with an image

Infamy and notoriety, power, money, and celebrities
If it wasn't for the treason, they'd be famous for no reason

Feel Me Up

Shuffle up and deal- I'm looking for a deal
Two for the price of one- That's a special kind of meal
Nothing good is cheap- I'm on a spending spree
Having twice the fun- So I buy one get one free

Please me, tease me, squeeze me,
Feel me up and hold me
Please me, tease me, squeeze me
Hurry up and love me

It's just a dime a dozen- I try to stay on budget
Time to shake and bake- So I put it in the oven
I try to stretch my money- And hold in my fat tummy
I get more for the bang- When I'm sweet to my honey

Please me, tease me, squeeze me,
Feel me up and hold me
Please me, tease me, squeeze me
Hurry up and love me

Fell Asleep

written 9-11-23

My family that I love will bring flowers to my grave
The sun will shine down when it rains on my parade
The earth will welcome me as the dirt covers up
The tears will gently roll left behind in the dust

Fell asleep like a log- Fell asleep like a rock
Fell asleep to the sounds of the tik of the tok

A mother sends a prayer and a child says goodbye
The grass will be greener on the other side
An X will mark the spot where my bones shall remain
The wind will bring a chill as it whistles out my name

Fell asleep like a log- Fell asleep like a rock
Fell asleep to the sounds of the tik of the tok

Finish What I Started

I just got back on my feet
Now I dance to my own beat
I make up my own pattern
And get wild in the street

Before I go back down in flames
I want to finish what I started
Climb my way back to the top
And get to the bottom of it

My hands are no longer tied
Now I can paint what I like
I can see what others don't
Like where the lightning strikes

Before I crash and burn again
I want to finish what I started
Keep my words dear to me
Is my funny way to say it

Some may think I'm arrogant- Some may think I'm quiet
But I know when to get going- And I know how to finish it
Some may get distracted- Some may get frustrated
I mat start off from behind- But I know how to finish it

Girl Dad

The times they are a changing and the clock is growing wings
I guess that's what I get on her way to age of eighteen

When I don't hear from her, I get a little sad
When she doesn't clean her room, I get a little mad

Yea I'm just a little girl's dad- She made it cool for me
To be a little girl's dad- Bounce her on my knee

The heart is just a giant muscle, and it cares more than it bleeds
I love to watch her sprout, growing up like the weeds

When I spend time with her, I feel a little glad
When I'm not beside her, I feel a little bad

Yea I'm just a little girl's dad- She made it cool for me
To be a little girl's dad- Bounce her on my knee

If she falls down in life, I'll be there to pick her up
If she flies and soras away, we will always be a duet

I'm just a little girl's dad, no matter how big she gets
I'm just a little girl's dad, that child, I will never forget

Give Me Your Last Name

Look into my eyes and see what you see
A glimpse into the future for you and me
Listen to your heart and hear what I say
I'd travel the world to get you to stay

I follow the rules, but I don't play games
Just tell me the score and give me your last name
If you say you love me, I'll tell you the same
Just show me how much and give me your last name

Touch my young soul and feel what you feel
The power of love is stronger than steel
Speak of true love and relish the taste
I'd give you the food right off of my plate

I follow the rules, but I don't play games
Just tell me the score and give me your last name
If you say you love me, I'll tell you the same
Just show me how much and give me your last name

Give Me Your Sympathy

I live in the big house on the bad side of town
I'm told when to wake up and when to lay back down
Got caught red handed with a full truck load
Of luxury brands and Hollywood gold

Don't judge me or fear me, just give me your sympathy
Don't blame me or hate me, just give me your sympathy

I live in the dungeon on the 3rd floor of hell
I have to fight for my rights in this death trap hotel
Chased by a nightmare in the heat of the day
All guns were a blazing, but I can't get away

Don't judge me or fear me, just give me your sympathy
Don't blame me or hate me, just give me your sympathy

I live life all alone 23 hours a day
Drink from a fountain and eat food from a tray
I'm guilty as charged for the crimes I commit
It was kill or be killed like Circus Maximus

God Of Chaos

written 12/23

Neither good nor evil- Playing tricks on me
The battle of the Republic- And the war on peace

I get lost and found- With nobody around
Like the God of chaos- When she strikes me down

God of Chaos- She's breaking the mold
God of chaos- She's out of control

Running out of time- The clock strikes noon
Death waits for us- Like the sun and the moon

I feel scared and lazy- A little foolhardy
Like the God of Chaos-
She hoodwinks the enemy

God of Chaos- She's breaking
the mold
God of chaos- She's out of
control

God Paints The Skies

The clouds block the sun and cast shadows of doubt
The rain breaks the levee and brings floods throughout
The winds blow the seeds on a distant sail voyage
Filled with twist and turns that aim to destroy ya

Select your weapon of choice and take your final breath
Cuz, you know in the end, you must fight to the death
God paints the pale sky with prismatic colors
And lifts up the world upon his broad shoulders

The eagles take flight over the deepest canyons
They swoop down on their catch like a Navy battalion
The children migrate hundreds to thousands of miles
Search for the breeding grounds and a soulmate to fertile

Choose your own path to follow and don't ever look back
Cuz, you know it wont matter, it will be a long rocky track
God paints the pale sky with prismatic colors
And lifts up the world upon his broad shoulders

God Plays Centerfield

written 8/15/23

You don't need to cut off your nose to save your face
You just need to open your eyes to take the embrace
You don't need to pretend that he's not enough
You just have to find your peace when things get tough

Thou shall not lie, covet, or steal
You don't have to lean left or right
God plays centerfield
Thou shall not cheat, commit, or kill
You don't have to be the best
God plays centerfield

You don't need to change your address to make yourself a home
You just need to open the door and make yourself be known
You don't have to hide your toys when you go to school
You just have to share them and play by all the rules

Thou shall not lie, covet, or steal
You don't have to lean left or right
God plays centerfield
Thou shall not cheat, commit, or kill
You don't have to be the best
God plays centerfield

Going Insane

written 11/4/23

I don't always understand my feelings- They just want to do their own things
Friday nights are my best time for healing- Talk about the things I must redeem

Times will come and times will go, and times will always tell
Am I going insane or going straight to hell
Whiskey glasses and whiskey jars and whiskey on my mind
Am I going insane or am I doing fine

We all want to paint the perfect picture- A masterpiece to show our better years
I try to live my life with scripture- The spirit helps my demons disappear

Times will come and times will go, and times will always tell
Am I going insane or going straight to hell
Whiskey glasses and whiskey jars and whiskey on my mind
Am I going insane or am I doing fine

Graveyard Of Empires

It takes a lifetime to build a nation but only a day to rip it apart
Constructed by a cast of heroes forged from inside the heart
My heroes come in many colors, odd shapes and size
They are the brave men and women that keep us safe at night

The graveyard of empires is no place for the wise
They shoot you down, blow you up and cut out your eyes

Many foes failed trying to conquer the iron gates
From Genghis Khan to Alexander the Great
The outsiders get distracted and never stay long enough
The warlords bunker down and call them at their bluff

The graveyard of empires is a trail of dust and bones
They pull you down, hang you up and crush you with the stones

Gym Rat

written 7/26/23

Wake up early
Eat my Wheaties
Break a sweat
Rest and repeat

Grunt and groan
Look at me
Strike a pose
Take a selfie

I'm not here to socialize, I'm not here to chit chat
I'm not your average Joe, I'm just the local gym rat

Guys take a look
You get nothing for free
If you work it hard
It's a possibility

Curls for the girls
Dumbbells and reps
Look at the mirror
Arms and chest

I'm not here to socialize, I'm not here to chit chat
I'm not your average Joe, I'm just the local gym rat

Happy Halloween

written 10/5/23

Happy Halloween
See the bodies bleed
Hear the children scream
It's a trick or treat

Steal the candy from the kids
Turn their smiles upside down
Dress them up like ghost
Paint their faces like a clown

Happy Halloween
Monsters start to creep
Pails of rotten teeth
It's a trick or treat

Little devils ring the bell
And witches rule the sky
They dominate the hood
On broomsticks they shall ride

Happy Halloween
Time to make believe
The dead roam the streets
It's a trick or treat

The sky is dark as hell
And the moon is shining bright
You can smell the fear
When werewolves howl at night

Head Over Heels

written 11/15/23

Her eyes can freeze you in your tracks
And her voice can tease you just like that
She's hotter than the sweet sunshine
Finer than a glass of wine

She fills my heart with little hearts
As Cupid shoots his little darts
Spinning circles round and round
Head over heels and upside down

When she walks into the room, I hear violins
And when she smiles the Angels sing
She's the gospel in my prayers
She' my little dancing bear

She fills my heart with little hearts
As Cupid shoots his little darts
Spinning circles round and round
Head over heels and upside down

Hell, Aint A Bad Place

written 11/3/23

I was born in hell and grew wild as a crazy horse
I eat nails for breakfast, and I spit on your corpse
I drink like a fish, and I swim like a dead rock
I'm the king of the jungle and I hunt around the clock

I live in the basement, but I live life for free
Hell, aint a bad place if you can stand the heat
I sleep in the corner like a cat with fleas
Hell, aint a bad place if you got hooves for feet

I was never a good lay, but I lie like a rug
I taste your sweet soul and I get high like a drug
I run with a rough crowd and my friends are in jail
I'm happy as a dog when I wag my pointed tail

I live in the basement, but I live life for free
Hell, aint a bad place if you can stand the heat
I sleep in the corner like a cat with fleas
Hell, aint a bad place if you got hooves for feet

Hellenbach

9-26-23

It's a slippery slope I travel, down the rabbit hole I go
I've been everywhere man, I'm at the end of my rope
I lost my money on a horse, at the dog and pony show
Fell off the wagon once before and met the edge of the road

I stayed when I should have left- Left when I should have stayed
Won when I should have lost- Lost when I should have played

My veins are cold as ice- As I place my bet on black
My life spins round and round- I've been to Hellenbach

I've met the devil face to face, looked him in the eye
Made a bet he had to take, then my bluff stole the prize
The goal post keeps changing and the score gets out of hand
I line up for the payoff, got outlived by the dammed

I stayed when I should have left- Left when I should have stayed
Won when I should have lost- Lost when I should have played

My veins are cold as ice- As I place my bet on black
My life spins round and round- I've been to Hellenbach

Hide And Seek

Lord, I can hear the silence and the calm before the storm
I can see the darkness and the clouds begin to form
Lord, I can feel the winds and the temperature increase
I can smell the blood from the raining in the streets

I can sense a sneak attack blowing from the East
Like a ghost in the graveyard, I hide and then I seek

Lord, I fought, and I climbed my way up from the gutter
I struggled many years but now I thrive and I prosper
Lord, you seen me at my worse, but you gave me another day
You pardoned my misdeeds and showed me the way

I'm hard to pin down like a child running free
Ready or not my friend, I hide and then I seek

Honey Bee

9/25/23

You made me smile- You made my day
The sky turns blue- And clouds clear away
You made me blush- You made my night
The flowers breathe- And brought to life

You made me love again- And my heart skip a beat
The music plays softly- When you treat me so sweet

Come on pretty baby- Come get to know me
Come on lovely lady- You can bee my honey

Come on pretty baby- Fly home with me
Come on lovely lady- You can bee my honey

You made me dream in color- You made my bed smell new
The curtains opened up- And it sparkled my view
You made me strong- You made my knees weak
The touch and the time- And love language speak

You made me your friend- And my trust become yours
The eyes of an angel- With a soul I procure

Come on pretty baby- Come get to know me
Come on lovely lady- You can bee my honey
Come on pretty baby- Fly home with me
Come on lovely lady- You can bee my honey

Huff And Puff

written 11/1/23

There's something to see- When she's ready to please
She opens the door and gets down on her knees
I travel alone- When I'm on the road
I play by myself- It's all part of the show

I hold my breath until my face turns blue
I push on my chest until my heart beats true
I huff and I puff until I can't see straight
I knock and I knock until she opens the gate

There's no one to blame- When I say the wrong name
I tickle her toes- But she already came
I work on my words- And my devotion to her
I tell her I'm sorry- And our flame still burns

I hold my breath until my face turns blue
I push on my chest until my heart beats true
I huff and I puff until I can't see straight
I knock and I knock until she opens the gate

Her weapon of choice- Is to silence my voice
So, I grab her fat ass- And I turn up the noise
I bite my own tongue- When she tells me I'm wrong
I sleep in the man cave- Then I go cut the lawn

I know You're All Alone

written 9-8-23

Now I don't go in the sunshine
I'm in the shadows of the night
I keep an eye on your bedroom
Behind the curtains out of sight

I'm the lead inside your pipes
In your dreams you can't deny
I keep a diary of your nightmares
So, I know you when you die

I'm breathing on the phone- I
know you're all alone
I steal away your soul- Like I did
to Al Capone
I'm living inside your home- I
know you're all alone
I eat away your soul- Heart, brain and bones

I'm the water when you bathe
In the photographs you take
My skin boils red
I watch until you wake

Your faith keeps you safe
From the hiss of the snakes
Like a lion in a cage
I wait for your mistake

I'm breathing on the phone- I know you're all alone
I steal away your soul- Like I did to Al Capone
I'm living inside your home- I know you're all alone
I eat away your soul- Heart, brain and bones

I'll Drink To That

Friday night at the pub, let the good times begin
The sound of country music, and the crowd welcomes you in
I've been working hard all week, now it's time to dust my brain
Whiskey, beer, and wine, and maybe a little cocaine

Pour me a double- Raise your glass
You know the words- I'll drink to that
Stand loud and tall- Raise the flag
You know the words- I'll drink to that

Just spent all my money on Jack, Jim and Juan
With friends like that, I can barely hang on
The band hits the stage and the songs they all rhyme
The girls laugh and dance, man they all look so fine

Just give me a reason and give me a bottle
It's too early to sleep, so I lay down that throttle
Yea the clock says 2am but it's my weekend off
I got nowhere else to be, no curfew and no boss

Pour me a another- Raise your glass
You know the words- I'll drink to that
Stand loud and tall- Take off your hat
You know the words- I'll drink to that

Imagine

Life needs to be sweeter, like pudding, sugar and spice
Bring more people together, like a cord that makes a splice
Follow your hopes and dreams, always pay attention
You may not know where to go, so use your imagination

A great man once said, imagine all the people, it's easy if you try
Come together, revolution, and a day in the life

We can search high and low, find a place on the map
Build a better way, like a bridge that fills a gap
Follow the road less traveled, meet your destination
A journey thru the wilderness, use your imagination

A great man once said, imagine all the people, living in peace
All you need is love and while my guitar gently weeps

It's All A Part Of Me

written 11/6/23

When I was a young man- I made friends for life
Moved away from home- And I found myself a wife
Every now and then- It's all I think about
The less I start to care- The less I do without

I did everything I did- To make sure I got ahead
It's all a part of me- It's all about the story

Now that I'm facing time- I start to look around
I wish I had the answers- To the things in life I found
Every now and then- It's all I think about
The more I start to gain- The more I do without

I took everything I took- To
make sure I got ahead
It's all a part of me- It's all
about the story

It's All Rock N Roll To Me

written 11/11/23

I was born in the 1970s when you had to dial in your tunes
I grew up metal as fuck but now I love my country and blues

I went to school in the 1980s when Prince and Aerosmith ruled the land
We parked the cars at the lake listening to our favorite bands

Power chords and cowboy chords, let the music set you free
Broken chords and altered chords, it's all rock n roll to me

It all got weird in the 1980s when the boy bands came out to play
I rebelled with some grunge, punk, hip hop, and reggae

Y2K started a new revolution and there aint no going back
No more Eddie or Dime no more back in black

Power chords and cowboy chords, let the music set you free
Broken chords and altered chords, it's all rock n roll to me

King Berserker

written 1/24

He lives in a castle with a pile full of diamonds and gold
He tells many stories of life and battles that never get old
His beard gets longer and grayer and his fingers swell and bleed
His hammer breaks flesh and bone with a sound that shocks the weak

He goes by many names- Mother of Pearl, God of Thunder, Master of Doom, King Berserker
He captures many flags- A loyal soldier, Holy warrior, Bringer of death, King Berserker

His book of shadows was a collection of brilliant yet wicked tales
His black label gang was destructive, loud and raised all hell
He comes down from the hills once a year to fight, steal and pillage
He eats the food and drinks all the beer and wine from the village

He goes by many names- Mother of Pearl, God of Thunder, Master of Doom, King Berserker
He captures many flags- A loyal soldier, Holy warrior, Bringer of death, King Berserker

Let's Be Friends Forever

written June 29, 2023

I met you when I was 10
Right from the start we were friends
We took on more than life
You had my back until the end

No matter where you are
No matter where you go
You always understand
What I mean and what I know

You're my Ace on the river
I am your King whatsoever
You're my Queen to my answer
Baby, let's be friends forever

You're my Heart thru the arrow
I'm your Diamond in the rough
You're my heat thru the Winter
Baby, let's be friends forever

I fought hard for your thoughts
You stole my heart from the start
I played games just to play
And the movie played my part

No wonder why I stare
No wonder why I care
You're always there for me
Thru the thick and thru the year

You're my Ace on the river
I'm your King whatsoever
You're my Queen to my answer
Baby, let's be friends forever

You're my Heart thru the arrow
I'm your Diamond in the rough
You're my heat thru the Winter
Baby, let's be friends forever

Life On The Road

written 7/9/23

The trouble with me is that I don't always see
The trouble I caused for my family

I run away- like a freight train
Ride them rails- I don't want to stay
Ride them rails- all night long
My mama calls- but I'm not around

My daddy's on the line- he is doing just fine
My sisters said- you need to make up some time

So, I thumbed my way- on the Blue Ridge Parkway
Life on the road- you can always come home
I'm on my way- I'm doing ok
Life on the road- you can always come home

The problem I have is that I don't feel bad
About the problems that make others sad

I fly high- like an eagle in flight
My wings are free- to do what I please
My wings are free- the sky is clear
My body calls- but I disappear

My daddy's on the line- he is doing just fine
My sisters said- you need to make up some time

So, I thumbed my way- on the blue ridge parkway
Life on the road- you can always come home
I'm on my way- I'm doing ok
Life on the road- you can always come home

Little Lady

written 10/8/23

I was the one who took you
And met with your first date
I watched you from a distance
As you put on roller skates

I wanted to come help you
And help tie your final lace
But I bit my lip on purpose
And gave you two some space

I wish I could press pause
And keep you home with me
But I love to watch you grow
And become a little lady

I love to see you walk
And skip ahead of me
You're my only Angel
Daddy's little lady

I kept my promise to you
But you knew I was close by
I was happy to see you smile
As I was crying on the inside

You know I'll always love you
And be there when you need
I'm always gonna be dad
Even when you're sixty

I wish I could press pause
And keep you home with me
But I love to watch you grow
And become a little lady

I love to see you walk
And skip ahead of me
You're my only Angel
Daddy's little lady

It made me feel special
When she asked if I liked him
So, I gave him a little fist pump
And she gave me a little grin

It was only 5 hours later
That I hinted we should go
My night went pretty cool
I think I handled it like a pro

Little Miss Understood

Her eyes said yes but her hand said no
She let me bleed and slapped my ego
Hush now baby, It's not all about you
I got places to go, and things to do

Sorry darling, my mistake
I'm a little miss understood
And you're a little too young for me to date

Her man walked up and looked me down
I said how's the weather and he looked around
Come on buddy, I tried to avoid you
I talk too much, and I had a few

Sorry Mr., My mistake
I'm a little miss understood
And a little too old to blame

Living In A Small Town
As God Smiled Down

written 8/15/23

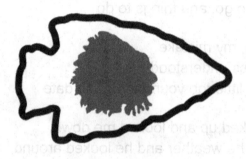

Legends and friends- Boys to men
Brothers in arms- And champions
Romans and Citizens- 4-3 defense
Monkey rolls- And winning traditions

There was a place and time, we felt safe and sound
Living in a small town, as God smiled down
We knew when it was dinner time, no more running around
Living in a small town, as God smiled down

Simpson and Johnson- Braves to Indians
Summer mohawks- And Wayne Jamison
Hinkle and Deegan- Cold beer and gin
Frosty windows- And Ford Mustangs

There was a place and time, we felt safe and sound
Living in a small town, as God smiled down
We knew when it was dinner time, no more running around
Living in a small town, as God smiled down

First and ten- Hit and spins
Mountaineer field- And overtime wins
It was REM- And Ultimate Sin
Growing up- In Slav's basement

Lucky Duck

written 8/11/23

My life has been a blessing and a curse
It's been a sweetheart deal but getting worse
I'm stuck in chains that can't be broke loose
I lost my horseshoe and my golden goose
It's been fine since I found my rabbit's foot
But not for the poor bastard's life that I took
I put my best foot forward from here on out
When I hear the devil's voice scream and shout
A trail of tears takes me back to the start
Uncharted grounds and many broken hearts

Break a leg- best of luck
Knock- em dead- you lucky duck

Find a penny- pick it up
Knock on wood you lucky duck

You know I was born under a bad sign
The teacher told my mom I wasn't kind
It was a rainy day at my parade
I was the kid that always disobeyed
I was the straw that broke my daddy's back
I felt the pain when I stepped into that crack
I've always been the toughest row to hoe
But I'm a tougher one to get to know

Break a leg- best of luck
Knock- em dead- you lucky duck
Find a penny- pick it up
Knock on wood you lucky duck

Magic Carpet Ride

written 10/20/23

My eyes have seen the glory of the beauty of this land
I swam the deepest oceans and put my toes in the sand
I climbed the tallest mountains and made friends along the way
I drove the rode to Hana and around the aloha State

Never saddle a dead horse, it won't take you anywhere
Find yourself a rocket ship and fly right of here

Take a shop, take a bus, take a detour in your life
Take a plane, take a train, take a magic carpet ride

My feet have climbed the stairs to the heavens and the clouds
Chased a girl around the globe but she lost me in Cape Town

I worshipped in a temple and ate shrimp on the barbie
Smoked weed with the locals and rescued a dog named Harley

Never saddle a dead horse, it won't take you anywhere
Find yourself a rocket ship and fly right of here

Take a shop, take a bus, take a detour in your life
Take a plane, take a train, take a magic carpet ride

Man Made

Sitting in the park in the middle of the day
Not a single worry as I watch the children play
The sky is blue, and the grass is green
I rest my eyes when the black bird sings

Riding with my windows down on A1A
Listening to the music sail across the ocean waves
The road is straight and many miles long
I find myself engaged and my troubles all gone

Every time I wake up, I definitely got it made
But I'm not a made man, I'm just a man that made his way

Hiking over the hills and thru the thicken woods
Stopping for the flowers that always smell so good
The path is clear, and the trees are tall
My favorite time is in the Fall

Working hard so I can live my life
Having fun and playing nice
The things that I keep so dear to me
Is the time I spend with my family

Every time I wake up, I definitely got it made
But I'm not a made man, I'm just a man that made his way

March Your Feet

written 8/6/23

When the sky starts to fall and there's no place left to hide
You better find your cross and get yourself in line
When the wall starts to crack, and it all comes crashing down
You better find your faith and sing it nice and loud

Left, right, left or somewhere in between
You better march your feet to the sound of the beat
Left, right, left or in the middle of the road
You better march your feet to the sound of the beat

When the clouds start to twist, and the wind blows your mind
You better find your church and get yourself inside
When the preacher man preaches about the end of time
You better find your God and get yourself enshrined

Left, right, left or somewhere in between
You better march your feet to the sound of the beat
Left, right, left or in the middle of the road
You better march your feet to the sound of the beat

Medusa

written 8/21/23

Run and hide and lock the gates
Even monsters have their place
They grab you tight, there's no escape
Some can even shift their shape

Cruel fate meets cruel intentions
Sweet dream and sweet emotions

You know I'm a snake, but you love the way I squeeze and bite
I know you're a witch, but I like the way you scratch and fight

Just like Medusa- I'm going to turn you to stone
Just like Medusa- You know I'm bad to the bone

A story of beauty, power, and betrayal
With resilience and symbol of survival
Lady of sorrow with a cursed love affair
Riding the shadows of the cold nighttime air

Cruel words meet cruel imagination
Sweet slurs and sweet exaggeration

You know I'm a snake, but you love the way I squeeze and bite
I know you're a witch, but I like the way you scratch and fight

Just like Medusa- I'm going to turn you to stone
Just like Medusa- You know I'm bad to the bone

Money Makes The World Go Round

Take me to your leader, I'm here to meet and greet
Stab you in the back and fill my ship with greed
I want to meet your King, I come to you in peace
All I want is your collection, the shiny, gold and green
I've been watching you for years pay all the taxes for me
You should know by now, nothing in this life is free

Around the world and around the globe- I'm going in circles
everywhere I go
Money makes the world go round- But the good and evil steal
the show

I'll leave you with a thought as I invade your sexy planet
If you want to survive, just give it up and quit
From the rivers in the West to the banks across the sea
I'd kill to have the power to maintain my spending spree
Your guts are inside out, the world is upside down
You disobey the laws that keep you safe and sound

Around the world and around the globe- I'm going in circles
everywhere I go
Money makes the world go round- But the good and evil steal
the show

Let me tell you about my travels, I've been down this road before
Indulgence is like a cancer; it keeps coming back for more
You know I speak the truth about the evil of your ways
You cannot do without; it eats at your decay

Mother May I

To find love, you must let love find you
It's only human to follow the clues
The lightning strikes and the thunder will crash
As the moon rises, the waves splash

Mother Nature, Mother Earth
Mother may I have this turn

Love the way I live, live the way I love
No one knows that better than the heaven above
The flowers bloom and the forest will grow
As the sun shines, the rivers flow

Mother Nature, Mother Earth
Mother may I have a turn

Music

written 10/25/23

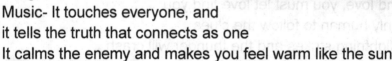

Melody, harmony, sensation- the
good stuff that I love to feel
Like a sound that travels thru air
It can be heard when it reaches
the ear

Music- it gives us peace and it
comes from the heart and soul
It keeps us going and helps us
not grow old
Music- It touches everyone, and
it tells the truth that connects as one
It calms the enemy and makes you feel warm like the sun

Energy, frequency, vibration- the good stuff that I love to hear
Like an expression that breaks the chains
It can be felt in your blood and veins

Music- it gives us peace and it comes from the heart and soul
It keeps us going and helps us not grow old
Music- It touches everyone, and it tells the truth that connects
as one
It calms the enemy and makes you feel warm like the sun

118

Never Enough

written 7/7/23

You can be my honey- You can be my friend
You can be my angel- Forgive me for my sins

Take me for my money- Take me for a fool
You can be the devil- Make me lose my cool

Life aint getting younger- It's only catching up
Got to feed my hunger- I never get enough
Life aint getting past us- It's only getting tough
Got to fill my pockets- I never get enough

Take me for a daydream- You can make a wish
Take me home to mama- Make my favorite dish

You can be my baby- I can be your man
You can say you love me- Make me understand

Life aint getting younger- It's only catching up
Got to feed my hunger- I never get enough
Life aint getting past us- It's only getting tough
Got to fill my pockets- I never get enough

Never Touch Another Man's Hat

written 11/28/23

Walk a mile in my shoes before you judge my ways
Have a drink with me first and hear what I have to say
I'm a rather quiet man, kind, gentle and polite
I can turn the other cheek; I know what's wrong from right

You can steal my sweetheart and try to kick my ass
You can even take what's mine but never touch another man's hat
Didn't anyone ever tell you that it's a matter of fact
You can dance with the devil but never touch another man's hat

You can leave dead or alive, makes no difference to me
I just want to finish my beer before I get down and dirty
These boots were made for kicking and this aint no wedding ring
I'll kill you with my kindness before I take a swing

You can steal my sweetheart and try to kick my ass
You can even take what's mine but never touch another man's hat
Didn't anyone ever tell you that it's a matter of fact
You can dance with the devil but never touch another man's hat

No One Will Miss Me

written 1/25/2024

I'm always the villain in the story, they never give me a better part
I'm the fight and confrontation in the shadow of the stars
I'm always the first one to die and the last to leave the scene
I've been slapped around and cut and got beat up by Steve McQueen

I ride like a desperado, and I fly like a kamikaze
I rebel like a renegade, but no one will ever miss me

No one will miss me- If I don't show up
No one will miss me- If I get hit by a truck

There's a bounty on my head and another battle to lose
I'll never live long enough to read all the reviews
The lights and cameras fade when I take my final breath
Forgiveness is my weakness as I fake my tragic death

I ride like a desperado, and I fly like a kamikaze
I rebel like a renegade, but no one will ever miss me

No one will miss me- If I fall thru the crack
No one will miss me- If I get shot in the back

Not The First Time

I just learned about my dear friend
She left in the still of the night
Traveling down that long dark road
To find herself the shining light

She had a kind and gentle soul
Friendlier than the kid next door
Much too young to leave this earth
Now she can't hug the trees anymore

It's not the first time I got burned and it won't be the last
Life can teach you many lessons and pass you by in a flash
It's not the first time I cried a tear, and it won't be the last
Living, breathing and being, affection, sorrow and laugh

It left an empty feeling inside me
From the moment that I heard
Freedom, nature and spirit
And sweet as a mama bird

I won't pretend to know the whole story
Or that I even knew her that well
But I know she loved her mother
And the way the flowers smell

It's not the first time I got burned and it won't be the last
Life can teach you many lessons and pass you by in a flash
It's not the first time I cried a tear, and it won't be the last
Living, breathing and being, affection, sorrow and laugh

One Drink, One Bet, And A Promise

written 10/29/23

The sun don't always shine and the clouds don't always rain
A drink won't hurt nobody, but it takes away the pain
And I don't always have to be the center of attention
I just keep my head on straight and take what life creates

If you wait here for me and you want me to be honest
I can keep my word to you with one drink, one bet, I promise
If you think I would lie to you and I lost your love and trust
I can make it up to you with one drink, one bet, I promise

The moon don't always rise and the river don't always crest
A bet can't make somebody, but it helps you beat the rest
And I don't always have to promise my true intentions
I just read all the faces and lean into my losses

If you wait here for me and you want me to be honest
I can keep my word to you with one drink, one bet, I promise
If you think I would lie to you and I lost your love and trust
I can make it up to you with one drink, one bet, I promise

The ball don't always hit the rim and the peg don't always fit
A rebound can't make someone but at least you didn't quit
And I don't have to be the winner or the loser
I'll just come back tomorrow and start my day all over

The wind don't always blow and the sky don't always fall
A promise can't break anyone but it hurts if it's recalled
And I don't always have to be the man, the myth, the legend
I can find my happy place and rest in my resting place

One Hell Of A Night

written 1/24

I walked into the bar all alone
to start my eve
I bumped into some friends
that wouldn't let me leave
The drinks were lining up on
the wet counter top
I made a bone to pick, and I
slammed my lemon drop

Women to the left- Women to
the right
I died and went to heaven for
one hell of a night
Angels to the left- Angels to
the right
I died and went to heaven for
one hell of a night

I met a girl named Rosie and her best friend Cherry Pie
I started telling stories and the laughter made them cry
Well, I couldn't believe my ears when they invited me back
home
I started feeling lucky then I grabbed my keys and phone

Women to the left- Women to the right
I died and went to heaven for one hell of a night
Angels to the left- Angels to the right
I died and went to heaven for one hell of a night

One More Shot

written 12/23

Well, the bartender knows my name and he knows what I like to drink
Mix me up some beauties and I end up with my face in the sink

I traded in my woman, and I threw in the towel
I'm feeling my age, but I still got my health

Give me one more shot- Give me one more day
Slip me another and I'll be on my way

Well, I'm not in the mood for talking, I'd rather sit around and whine
Fire me up some dragons, loosen the goose and feel fine

I let my beard grow long and my hair turn grey
Listening to the sounds of my yesterday

Give me one more shot- Give me one more day
Slip me another and I'll be on my way

One Trick Pony

I may not be a dark horse, but I sure know how to lead the way
I may not be a jack of all trades, but I know how to play the game

If you want to ride along babe, you better try to get to know me
Cuz I'm not fooling anyone, I'm a one trick pony
If you want it more than once babe, you can cry, beg and plea
Cuz I'm not fooling anyone, I'm a one trick pony

I may not live in a golden corral, but I do like all you can eat
I may not ride with a saddle, but I will let you sit on my seat

If you want to ride along babe, you better try to get to know me
Cuz I'm not fooling anyone, I'm a one trick pony
If you want it more than once babe, you can cry, beg and plea
Cuz I'm not fooling anyone, I'm a one trick pony

Path Of Destruction

Living in a house of cards
Ready to Collapse
Teetering on the edge
My walls about to crack

I got a million-dollar view
From my back yard deck
There's a storm on the rise
My ship about to wreck

Lightning, wind and hail, chaos and disruption
Like hurricanes and cyclones, I leave a path of destruction

Finally reached a boiling point
My temper crossed the line
The circuits blew a fuse
Situation in decline

The sun is burning hot
Like when I am seeing red
I've been told a hundred times
To always count to ten

Lightning, wind and hail, chaos and disruption
Like hurricanes and cyclones, I leave a path of destruction

Perfect Mate

Things must change if you want them to stay the same
You must take the pain if you want to grow and gain

Birds of the same feather, all flocking together, finding their
own way
Yes, you got to weather the storm if you want to find the perfect
mate

Lovebirds fall in love like a hand in a glove
Singing like a dove in the blue skies above

Soldiers line up in order, all marching together, making it thru
the day
Yes, you got to weather the storm, if you want to find the perfect
mate

Pineapple Express

written 11/25/23

My life is like a rollercoaster- Keep on riding until it's over
My life is like an elevator- Always a new floor to explore

Apple pie and creamy delights
Extra sweet with a big surprise
Take a ride on the Pineapple Express
Like eating ice cream without the mess

Stir the bowl and batter up
Take a swing and lick the cup
Take a ride on the Pineapple Express
Like getting married without the stress

My life is like a bottle of wine- When I age, I get more fine
My life is like a contractor- Long screws and a big hammer

Apple pie and creamy delights
Extra sweet with a bug surprise
Take a ride on the Pineapple Express
Like eating ice cream without the mess

Stir the bowl and batter up
Take a swing and lick the cup
Take a ride on the Pineapple Express
Like getting married without the stress

Ponytails And Butterflies

written 11/2/23

I wish my day with you could last a lifetime and my nights were tangled in your hair
I wish I could fly you to Paris, France and we could have a midnight affair

Resourceful, strong and patient- Joyful, gracious and empathetic

Ponytails and butterflies- Berry sweet and angel eyes
Ponytails and butterflies- Magic wands and puppy cries

I hope that you could read my mind and lend your sweet ears to me
I hope that you can understand when I whisper to you my dreams

Humorous, serene and sensitive- Articulate, bold and enthusiastic

Ponytails and butterflies- Berry sweet and angel eyes
Ponytails and butterflies- Magic wands and puppy cries

You got me on my feet again- Danced to my favorite song
You taught me how to tango- And shook me all night long

Popcorn And A Movie

written 8/1/23

Sex, drugs, and rock and roll, money power, I got it all
Cocaine, hash, menage trois, big city lights and movie stars

Breaking out of my prison stripes, hanging out with all the whites
I'm tired of all those glamour nights, autographs and neon lights

Feeling kind of lazy, feeling kind of groovy
I just want to lay down with some popcorn and a movie

Tattoo darlings and chasing drinks, dragon, demons, and slinging ink
Rounding 3rd and headed home, come on in but I'm not alone

Social butterflies singing in my ear, Redefined man now I'm a cavalier
I don't want to be there, hibernate and disappear

Feeling kind of lazy, feeling kind of groovy
I just want to lay down with some popcorn and a movie

Dancing on the ceiling, painting the town red
Let's get this party started, cocktails in my bed
The show must go on, don't leave me here uptight
Need a place to unwind, that's the story of my life

Pot Of Gold

written 11/2/23

I am the native son- I am the wind
I am the chosen one- With tattooed skin
I hunt the open land- I bury man
I rule with iron fist- With just one hand
I squint to see- I am a chief
I am a warrior- My spirits free

Not every root gives birth to grass- Not every valley is on the map
A lesson learned is a lesson told- A pot of fools is a pot of gold

I chisel convicts- I ambush bandits
I aim and squeeze- My guns don't miss
I have no name- I pray for rain
I am the thunder- That brings the pain
I worship peace- I fly with geese
I pay attention- When wise men speak

A river cries a hundred tears- My blood has poured a thousand years
A lesson learned is a lesson told- A pot of fools is a pot of gold

Promise Them Tomorrow

written 12/7/23

Their religion is their religion, and it tells them what to do but they lie, and they lie and believe they are true

History- Geography
English and Biology

Take away what you will and learn what you can
Promise them tomorrow and teach them how to plan

Promise them tomorrow and what the prophet said
Promise them tomorrow and the days that lay ahead

Their story is their story, and it reads them like a book but the print on the paper isn't worth a second look

Chemistry- Philosophy
Drama and Ideology

Take away what you will and learn what you can
Promise them tomorrow and teach them how to plan

Promise them tomorrow and what the teacher said
Promise them tomorrow and the days that lay ahead

Ray Of Sunshine

(dedicated to my friend Rae)

She rode in on a glimmer of hope and danced around like a
feather blowing in the wind-
Young at heart but full of wisdom

Held down by gravity but lifted by spirit
Around the globe without any limits

The ray of light and glowing ghost
A ray of sunshine in the fog and smoke

She was cool, smooth, and fresh and flowed free like the water
in the Juniper springs-
Sounding like the music that nature sings

Detained by no one but nowhere to go
Searching for a family and to find a home

The ray of light and glowing ghost
A ray of sunshine that lived alone

Ring Around The Rosie

written 11/25/23

Come on honey- Come on down to see me
I don't really bite- I'm just like a puppy

Show me what you got- I'll tell you that you're hot
We can fly to Vegas- Tie the biggest knot

Ring around the Rosie- No excuse for being lonely
Got a bank filled with money- And my pockets full of ***y
Ring around the Rosie- You think you really know me
Got a rep for being naughty- And a bed that's nice and cozy

Come on baby- You look so fine and pretty
Underneath that dress- I want to pet your kitty

Hey sexy lady- You make me feel all dizzy
When you look me in the eyes- And tell me that you love me

Ring around the Rosie- No excuse for being lonely
Got a bank filled with money- And my pockets full of ***y
Ring around the Rosie- You think you really know me
Got a rep for being naughty- And a bed that's nice and cozy

Romancing The Stone

written 8/18/23

When I was a young kid, I used to run from kisses and hugs
But when I turned 17, I learned how to scratch those itches
I took advice from the new kids on the block
I watched Showtime around the clock

I can hear you groan when you're giving the dog a bone
I can hear you moan when you're romancing the stone

When I was 13, I took an interest in the opposite sex
But when I turned 21, I began to legally inject
It was like taking candy from a kid
It was like snatching babies from a crib

I can hear you groan when you're giving the dog a bone
I can hear you moan when you're romancing the stone

When I started getting old, I began to feel my age
So, I found a little pill to stiffen me up on stage
The audience said the show must go on
So, I cast a spell with my magic wand

Sad Prison Blues

written 11/28/23

I'm not here to make friends but I know how to survive
I do what I have to do in order to stay alive
I went to dinner and a show, but I did nothing wrong
I was totally framed, and I really don't belong

Locked up and tied down at the age of 22
Stripes on my shirt- I got the sad prison blues
Bank robbers, crazy killers, and homemade tattoos
Teardrops on my face- I got the sad prison blues

I feel out of breath like I'm trapped under ice
Live like a cockroach when they turn out the lights

Serving time in jail for a crime I did not commit
I got 15 to 20 but the glove does not fit

Locked up and tied down at the age of 22
Stripes on my shirt- I got the sad prison blues
Bank robbers, crazy killers, and homemade tattoos
Teardrops on my face- I got the sad prison blues

Santa Is Real

written 12/23

I've been a Santa for almost 21 years
I've sweated many nights and shredded lots of tears

But I'd do it all again just to wake up warm and toasty
Watching my honey child open presents in front of me

I know how you may feel but I think Santa is real
I know what you may think but hear me out wink-wink

Santa is real- he is the real deal
How else can you explain all the joy Christmas morning brings

I've seen the magic that I could never afford
Spent more time than I wanted at the five and dime store

If you desire something more then try to make believe
That the people who love you put those gifts under the tree

A father and mother can make you feel
Well to me that is something real

I know how you may feel but I think Santa is real
I know what you may think but hear me out wink-wink

Santa is real- he is the real deal
How else can you explain all the joy Christmas morning brings

Satisfaction Guaranteed

written 8/25/23

I'd like to buy the world a beer and drink all night
with me
I'd like to toast to happiness and goodwill to those
we meet
I'd like to shake the devil's hand and introduce my
name
I'd like to offer him a deal and beat him at his own game

I'd like to give DC some coke and bring them to
their knees
I'd like to see them all choke and keep our nation free
I'd like to tell them where to go and throw away
the key
I'd like to line them in a row, satisfaction guaranteed

I'd like to rob the tiger's stripes and give it to a deer
I'd rather teach my dog to hunt than to live his life in fear
I'd like to make a plan for war and bring peace to the land
I'd rather stand for allegiance than to bow to your commands

I'd like to give DC some coke and bring them to their knees
I'd like to see them all choke and keep our nation free
I'd like to tell them where to go and throw away the key
I'd like to line them in a row, satisfaction guaranteed

Scar Giver

written 12/23

In the cold shadows of the night where the strange bellies feed
Behind the dark silhouettes, a mad man walks the streets

A doctor of pain and merciful fate
A soldier of death with marks on his face

A stone-cold killer like Jack the Ripper
A preacher of doom and a scar giver

Silent nights with echoes of cobblestone where the mist slowly creeps
Got you in a stranglehold, drain your soul as you bleed

A doctor of pain and merciful fate
A soldier of death with marks on his face

A stone-cold killer like Jack the Ripper
A preacher of doom and a scar giver

Scaredy Cat

written 9/22/23

Hey lady of the night- I saw you float by my bed
I was too afraid to move- To coalesce with the dead

I felt your hand tap my shoulder- I saw your eyes touch my soul
I laid still as a whisper- And your hair was black as coal

I read your story from a book- And your writings on the wall
They say your spirit travels well- Passing buoyant down the hall

Nothing ever seemed so real- I thought I was wide awake
But my sleep was just a dream- And my brain was a mistake

I think I smell a rat
I play blind as a bat

Aint no hocus pocus
I'm just a scaredy cat

I heard you in the kitchen- Making sounds in the night
My body was frozen stiff- And my room cold as ice

I think it was just the wind- Or the wicked ice machine
The house was just unsettling- Too terrified to scream

I think I smell a rat
I play blind as a bat
Aint no hocus pocus
I'm just a scaredy cat

Scratch And A Dent

Remember that night I drove thru the gate
What a bad way to end our first date
Now you've been gone for way too long
I miss riding along to my favorite song

The damage is done form that night of fun
I hope you forgive me my big, bad half ton

A dent and a scratch- A smash and a crash
One wrong decision- Cost me thousands in cash

I know it can hurt but I never meant harm
You saw the red flags, all the signs and alarms
Forgive me my darling, my honey, my ride
I lost all direction; I shout and I cried

The pain is surreal, it takes time to heal
Hardship and agony, a trial and ordeal

A dent and a scratch- A smash and a crash
One little mistake- Cost me a week and a half

She's a Diamond

written 8/8/23

I found her all alone at
the end of a rainbow
Shining like a light
thru an open window

She holds my hands
and thoughts with a
magic touch
And paints her art
on the canvas with a
feather brush

She's a diamond in the rough- More valuable than gold
Warms my heart in the Winter- Like a fire when it's cold

I call to her in the midnight sun- To let her know I'll be home
I do my best to keep her safe- Like a castle made of stone

I wrote to her my poems on a fancy note
Drew her a life that we love to share the most

She plays the part of the sweet angel singing
With a voice that reminds me of a church bell ringing

She's a diamond in the rough- More valuable than gold
Warms my heart in the Winter- Like a fire when it's cold

I call to her in the midnight sun- To let her know I'll be home
I do my best to keep her safe- Like a castle made of stone

She's Just Like Her Daddy

written 11/30/23

Wouldn't you like to go back to that day
Back to the time that you had time to play
Remember when he showed you how to string a fishing pole
And he came to your games and saw you score your first goal

One day she will grow up and try to explain it
What that man did to prepare and assist

She's just like her daddy- stubborn as a mule and a little bit sassy
She's just like her daddy- smart, funny and a little bit crappy

Wouldn't you like to hear his voice get rough
Hey gosh darn it, its time to wake up
Remember when he taught you had to ride a skateboard
And he told you how to honor and believe in the lord

One day she will grow up and try to understand it
What she learned will make her someone else's gift

She's just like her daddy- stubborn as a mule and a little bit
sassy
She's just like her daddy- smart, funny and a little bit crappy

She Don't Know Defeat

I once stood between a dragon and her wrath
but that cost me more lives than my dog and my cat
Every part of this creature has a shield made from daggers
with teeth sharp as knives and claws like scissors

Screech and howl, scream and shout
Chew me up and spit me out

Even with all the love in the world, you can't tame a beast
She will never give in, she don't know defeat

I threw down my arms and pleaded for mercy
but she melted my sword and roared with a fury
A symbol of evil and astonishing power
She took over my castle and burned down my tower

Squawk and crawl, fight, and brawl
Show my hand and then withdraw

Even with all the love in the world,
you can't tame a beast
She will never give in, she don't
know defeat

Shred You Like A Doll

written 10-7-23

I try to do what's right in life
And make the right decisions
I don't need to get locked up
Or spend my life in prison

I'm the camel that broke your back
I'm not the shortest straw
Just because I bow my head
Don't mean I don't have claws

I'm nice, gentle and oh so sweet
I'm kind to one and all
But if you back me into a corner
I will shred you like a doll

I smile, hug and kiss oh so sweet
I'll lick you like a dog
But if you push me way too far
I will shred you like a doll

I try to follow all the rules
And elevate my position
I don't need to trick myself
Or get fooled by a magician

I'm the cat that got out of the bag
I'm happy with just a ball
Just because I don't start fights
Don't mean I don't have claws

I'm nice, gentle and oh so sweet
I'm kind to one and all
But if you back me into a corner
I will shred you like a doll

I smile, hug and kiss oh so sweet
I'll lick you like a dog
But if you push me way too far
I will shred you like a doll

Single Mama

Single mothers, tattoos, and dreams
Two full time jobs, and a load of jeans
9 to 5 and a boss in your ear
From overtime to mom of the year
Watch them babies and hold them tight
Help them learn and grow up right

You raised a small army all alone
Went to war each day on your own
You never ran from a hard luck fight
You been a single mom all your life

Cleaning, cooking, and little toy bins
Raising daughters and rugged boy twins
16 years since you been on a date
But you still know how to dress up great
Don't need no man to pay your bills
You got car keys and your own free will

You raised a small army all alone
Went to war each day on your own
You never ran from a hard luck fight
You been a single mom all your life

Soccer, dance, and baseball fields
Taxi driver to happy meals
Your spider senses are never wrong
You keep them safe where they belong
You ask for nothing and wrap the gifts
You walk the walk and never quit

Something To Believe In

written 11/24/23

We all keep chasing ghost-
something that is not real
Running down the memories-
of the things we used to feel
There has to be a reason- a
reason unknown to me
Something to believe in-
something that lives and
breathes

Give me pine trees, rivers and
mountains
A road map from where I've been
Give me good times, family and friends
Give me something to believe in

What is this place that you speak of- somewhere deep in the
woods
Searching for what we have lost- and things we misunderstood
There has to be a good cause- a cause undisclosed to me
Something for us to believe in- something that we can touch
and see

Give me blue ridge, wild and wonderful
A road map from where I've been
Give me good times, family and friends
Give me something to believe in

Stop, Listen, Learn, Start, Begin

written 7/10/23

Sometimes I just want to hibernate-
disappear from the grid
Sometimes I just want to alienate- fly
away in the wind
Sometimes I can be useless- and not
say a word
Sometimes I can be silent- still and
reserved

Stop and listen to my dreams
Learn to see what is real
Start to tell my own story
Begin to express what I feel

Sometimes I just want to isolate- separate from the rest
Sometimes I just want to annihilate- utterly destroy the past
Sometimes I can be angered- and preach with a rage
Sometimes I can be disturbed- with fury and craze

Stop and listen to my dreams
Learn to see what is real
Start to tell my own story
Begin to express what I feel

Sunday Morning

written 7/16/23

The sun is shining down, and the leaves are piling up
Another Sunday morning to fill my coffee cup
The T.V. shows are on, and the paper brings the news
Another Sunday morning on my porch with a view

Life can be exhausting, hard yet self-rewarding
Prepping for the week, just another Sunday morning
Life can be enduring, tough and yet refreshing
Looking for days ahead, just another Sunday morning

The birds are singing prayers, and the kids are sleeping in
Another Sunday morning to read my book in bed

The wind smells like rain and the house feels like a home
Another Sunday morning to spend with you alone

Life can be exhausting, hard yet self-rewarding
Prepping for the week, just another Sunday morning
Life can be enduring, tough and yet refreshing
Looking for days ahead, just another Sunday morning

Sweet And Sassy

written 12/23

She's the rain in the puddle that is always there
She knows my weaknesses and she really cares
She's the light in the tunnel that leads the way
She is my favorite show at the end of the day

She is sweet and sassy
Full of sunshine and makes me happy
She is sweet and sassy
A little bit sour but always classy

She's the shooting star that brings my wish
She is the tricky spot on me that I like to itch
She's the ocean breeze that cools my mind
She is the sea and shells and is all mine

She is sweet and sassy
Full of sunshine and makes me happy
She is sweet and sassy
A little bit sour but always classy

Sweet Emotion

written 7/21/23

Together our life begins
Touching and holding hands
Over the highest mountain
Around the sharpest bends

Now that we are bound together
And our lives have been set in motion
The search is finally over
We swell in the devotion

Now that we no longer sleep alone
And time with you has my attention

The rock has met his stone
Child-like sweet emotion

Together we ride the winds
Flying to distant lands
Sailing leeward on the ocean
Tracking course off the fringe

Now that we are bound together
And our lives have been set in motion
The search is finally over
We swell in the devotion

Now that we no longer sleep alone
And time with you has my attention
The rock has met his stone
Child-like sweet emotion

Sweet Sixteen

written 8/19/23

All my life, I wanted to grow up
Now, I'm past my prime with no luck
Can't blame my childhood, I had it good
Can't blame my teachers that I misunderstood

Remember the days we had it all
George, John, Ringo, and Paul

Sweet 16- Ready to please
I love them all to smithereens
Sweet 16- Dancing queen
I'm a rock and roll time machine

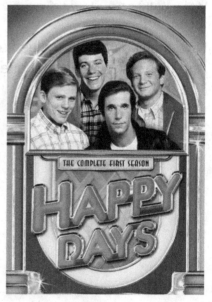

When I was cutting the rug, they called it the jitterbug
Now, I'm at the doctor asking for the strongest drugs
I want more than happy days on the couch
I want a boat, camper, and a two story house

Remember the days we had it all
Ralph, Richie, Potsie, and the Fonz

Sweet 16- Ready to please
I love them all to smithereens
Sweet 16- Dancing queen
I'm a rock and roll time machine

Take Me Home Again

written 1-24

Sitting around bored as fuck, playing music from the 70s
Hanging with some old friends, Jim, Jack, and my buddies
I aint too proud to cry in my beer, I know all the songs from
the 80s
Back when I drove a Camaro and communicated with the ladies

Bottoms up- Take me home again
Ride the wave- When my life began

One night in the middle of the night, I dreamed I was a legend
from the 90s
I asked Jesus for some directions, on my way to New York City
Once the smoke finally cleared, I was still breathing in the
2020s
The face in the mirror looked me in the eye, the voice said I
was sitting pretty

Bottoms up- Take me home again
Ride the wave- When my life began
Bottoms up- Take me home again
I'm still a baby- Where my life began

Take My Hand

written 9-12-23

The taste is sweet, so I sink my teeth
And bite into your flesh
The smell is quaint, so I sniff the paint
And keep you clean and fresh

Take my hand, I'm in command
I'll lead you here and there
Take my hand, I'm in demand
I'll lead you everywhere

The chase is great, so I take the bait
And make a date for two
The ride is fast, so I find a match
And prove my love to you

Take my hand, I'm in command
I'll lead you here and there
Take my hand, I'm in demand
I'll lead you everywhere

Take No Prisoners

written 11/24/23

If you want to know where it comes from then lay down with me tonight
I'll send you to another kingdom and take you on a wild flight
If you want to see something special, then look into my brown eyes
I'll show you how to grow wings and ride the enchanted skies

I will take no prisoners and free your inner child
Turn your fears to pleasure and dial in your smile
I will take no prisoners and free you from the guards
Open up the pathway and greet you with the charms

If you want to get to know me better, then show me that you believe
You can do anything you want, just ask and you shall receive
If you want to feed the dragon, then just close your eyes and see
Hold your hand out high and you will begin to hear him breathe

I will take no prisoners and free your inner child
Turn your fears to pleasure and dial in your smile
I will take no prisoners and free you from the guards
Open up the pathway and greet you with the charms

Take Your Best Shot

written 11/12/23

Driving down the interstate- blind as a bat
Hands on the steering wheel there's something in the back
Naked as a jailbird and happy as a clam
Squirrelly as a monkey but strong as a man

Take your best shot mama- If you're feel the need
I'll give you the house and sign over the deed
Take your best shot mama- If you got the balls
I'll give you the business, but I won't break the law

Headlights behind me- roadblocks ahead
I just want to get home and get in my bed
Long blonde hair blowing in the wind
Can't see the future but I bet you I win

Take your best shot mama-
If you're feel the need
I'll give you the house and
sign over the deed
Take your best shot mama-
If you got the balls
I'll give you the business,
but I won't break the law

Tell Me Something

written 11/15/23

I wake up in the morning and I make it thru the day
I come home to silence, but I have something to say

The snow is getting deeper, and the ice is getting thin
I'm searching for the answer of what may lay within

Tell me something to die for, I'll give you a minute to think
Make it something tasteful and I'll buy you another drink

I sip and stir my coffee and I eat my Raisin Bran
I read the local paper, but I don't understand

The sun is getting hotter, and the days are getting long
I'm searching for direction where do I belong

Tell me something to live for, I'll give you a second to think
Make it something respectful and I'll buy you another drink

Thank My Family and Friends (ride in the wind)

written 11/1/23

I take a ride down the highway, never gonna stay in my lane
My heart was feeling heavy, never gonna get her to stay

I'm feeling bitter, I'm feeling strange, I'm never gonna forget her name
I'm feeling nervous, I'm feeling aches, I'm never gonna give up the chase

I thank my family, I thank my friends, they made me feel welcome again
I thank my family, I thank my friends, they said I need to ride in the wind

I got my note from the doctor, got to learn to cope with the pain
My fevers getting higher, now I got to deal with the strain

I'm feeling empty, I'm feeling drained, I'm never gonna fill up
the space
I'm feeling worried, I'm feeling aged, now I got to make my
own way

I thank my family, I thank my friends, they made me feel
welcome again
I thank my family, I thank my friends, they said I need to ride
in the wind

That's The Girl

I need a girl that can steal the show, so I can sit back and watch her go
Don't tell me where to go or what to do, cuz chasing the dragon is nothing new
I've seen her prance, I've seen her move, rock this town and shake a groove
Yea she knows just what to do, drive me crazy and break the rules

That's the girl I'm looking for, so I can shut my window and open her door
That's the girl I'm looking for, loves to please and say yes sir

Pretty as a painting, bold as a lion, sweet as cherries and hot as an iron
Be my best friend so I'm never alone, give me warmth, shelter and take me home
She knows I like it when she takes the stage with adorables that are half her age
High heels, long hair and leopard shirt, red lips, angel face and leather skirt

That's the girl I'm looking, takes what I give and comes back for more
That's the girl I'm looking for, loves to please and say yes sir

I always know when she enters the room, the lights come on and my heart goes boom
She rules the night and owns the sky like a falcon hunts and the eagles fly

That's the girl from my dreams, makes me want to go back to sleep

The Circus

written 12/6/23

Tents, trapeze, and animal acts- Jugglers, clowns and acrobats
Come inside and join my class- I offer more than paid contracts

I fly above and crawl below- I've taken more than a million souls
I get so high then I get so low- That's just the way the circus goes

The children play and laugh out loud- As lion tamers please the crowd
The devils' music makes lovely sounds- Traps the audience in a foggy cloud

I saw you saw me, so I had to go- Before you got to say hello
I dance around and I steal the show- That's just the way the circus goes

The Good, The Bad,
And The Ugly

written 11/5/23

Well, I drink captain and coke and I
don't mind a good smoke
I'm like a bar fly on the wall, I hang
around until last call
I like to play my favorite songs and
sing with friends until dawn
I'm like a fish out of water when the
lights turn back on

I can be sweeter than a sugar pie
On a river full of honey
I can be mean as a killer outlaw
I'm like the good, the bad and the ugly

Well, I spend my credit fast cuz I keep running out of cash
I'm like a deer in the headlights when I see that final price
I like buying drinks all night and I don't mind a good fight
I'm like a wolf in sheep's clothing when I kick, scratch and bite

I can be sweeter than a sugar pie
On a river full of honey
I can be mean as a killer outlaw

I'm like the good, the bad and the ugly

Well, I like to show off my good taste, you know I love a pretty face
I'm like music to your ears when I'm spreading my good cheer
I like rolling the dice and scotch whiskey on ice
I'm like an ace up the sleeve when the dealer isn't nice

The One That Got Away

written 11/15/23

Back in school
I knew all the rules
But I played the fool
And lost my cool

Mistakes, I made a few
God willing, I swear to you

Take me back to yesterday where the
birds fly free and the children play
Take me back to yesterday to find my
past and the one that got away

Long brown hair
With skin so fair
The perfect flare
And a heart so rare

Hook line and sinker
Lord, I should have married her

Take me back to yesterday where the birds fly free and the
children play
Take me back to yesterday to find my past and the one that
got away

The Only Thing I Got To Do

written 9-2-23

Half past ten, I'm at the 7-Eleven, on Locust Avenue
Half past noon, I'm at the College Lunch, about to read the news
Half past five, almost time, I'm at the front of the line

No class today, it's my time to play, can't make the grade

The only thing I got to do is wake up and find my shoes
The only thing I got to do is hit the alarm clock snooze

Half past three, I'm at the Nautilus, getting on my boost
Half past six, I'm in Dirks backyard, drinking gin and juice
Half past nine, time to grind, I'm about to get mine

No class today, it's my time to play, can't make the grade

The only thing I got to do is wake up and find my shoes
The only thing I got to do is hit the alarm clock snooze

The Pub (Celebration)

written 8/5/23

I'm eating and drinking and smoking cigars
I'm dealing and winning and playing my cards
I'm humming and singing and strumming guitar
I'm giggling and fidgeting at the end of the bar

It may be dark, it's never too far, but at the Pub, I'm a pop star
It may be dark, it's never too far, but at the Pub, I'm a rock star

I'm talking and hanging with my degenerate friends
I'm fighting and brawling and busting heads
I'm flirting and smiling and touching women
I'm leaning and yawning and ready for bed

It may be dark, it's never too far, but at the Pub, I'm a pop star
It may be dark, it's never too far, but at the Pub, I'm a rock star

The Real Me

written 9-16-23

Let me tell you a story about the
time I ran away
I can be hard to find sometimes
when I don't get my own way
I'm not done with you if I haven't
thrown you out
I don't have a devil's bone, but I
can be mean with no sound

I can be stubborn as an ass and
dirty as a pig
Bite like a shark and hide like a
tick

The real me is deep inside, it
sleeps within and peaks for light
The real me is deep inside, it's nice to meet, the pleasure is
mine

Let me tell you something about the way you make me feel
I could bug the hell out of you by just keeping my lips sealed
You're not part of my plan if I haven't invited you in
But you can cook me dinner and I'll buy you a night of sin

I can be sweet as a kitten or a blank silhouette
Fake as a wig or as real as it gets

The real me is deep inside, it sleeps within and peaks for light
The real me is deep inside, it's nice to meet, the pleasure is mine

The School Of Hard Knocks

written 1-24

Let me tell you a story about the time I went to Vegas
I went there for the shopping but then things got outrageous
I woke up cold and numb in a bathtub full of ice
My clothes were neatly folded, and my back was stitched up nice

What doesn't kill me makes me stronger- I'm from the school of hard knocks
I had my share of bumps and bruises- Yea I've been around the block

The last thing I remember was the hookers and the coke
I gave them lots of money and they laughed at all my jokes

I guess things could be worse, I could have woken up dead
They left me a doctors note, at the end of my bed

What doesn't kill me makes me stronger- I'm from the school
of hard knocks
I had my share of bumps and bruises- Yea I've been around
the block

I think I'm going to live but I could have died alone
If it wasn't for the maid that heard me moan and groan
Several years have passed since I went under the knife
I still drink, smoke and gamble and I live a normal life

What doesn't kill me makes me stronger- I'm from the school
of hard knocks
I had my share of bumps and bruises- Yea I've been around
the block

The Secrets Of The Obscure

written 8/24/23

My mind is smarter than my brain and my brain is driving me insane
Running from the storm, caught in a hurricane

Trying to wrap my head- To help me understand
The secrets of the obscure- I'm trying to comprehend

My eyes can't see past the horizon and my horizon is my vision
Running for the hills, caught in an illusion

It looks like my perception- Is causing my confusion
The secrets of the obscure- A strange revelation

My soul is blacker than a shadow and my shadow is my home
Running from myself, caught in a hole

I'm in a fog of a condition- Diagnosed by my depression
The secrets of the obscure- Puzzled by imagination

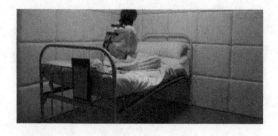

The Show Must Go On

written 1/24

Violence can be such an eye opener
Look around and enjoy the show
Life is like a breath of fresh air
It picks you up and then off you go

Hurry hurry- Step right up- The show must go on
Hurry hurry- No matter what- The show must go on

War is not for the weak at heart
It numbs your brain and tugs your soul
Death is like a punch in the gut
First you fall and then you choke

Hurry hurry- Step right up- The show must go on
Hurry hurry- No matter what- The show must go on

The Way Life Goes

written 10/31/23

If you wake the giant little boy, you better start to run
If you poke the bear little girl, you better have a gun
If you want a job little boy, you better go to school
If you play the game little girl, you better not get fooled

It's no cake walk or stroll in the park- It's not like leapfrog or throwing darts
It's the way life goes when you least expect- It's the little things you do that gain respect

If you bark up the wrong tree little boy, you better learn to fight
If you sleep around little girl, you better turn off the lights
If you grow fast little boy, you better tell the truth
If you find a penny little girl, you better have a clue

It's not freeze tag or two hand touch- It's not like teatime or having brunch
It's the way life goes when you least expect- It's the little things you do that gain respect

If you fall back down, you better get back up
If you aim to win, you better hit the cup

The Zone

written 11/18/23

Well, they don't care if you starve and sleep in the rain
They don't care if you beg and cry from the pain
They just want to pretend they know what to do
They just want to keep you hidden and away from the news

I'm here to tell you, you need to pick up and move
I'm here to tell you, you are not alone
There's a feeling of being old, worn, and tired here in the zone
No future at all, here in the zone

Well, they don't care if you sink and fall in the sea
They don't care if you cough or die from disease
They just want to look smart and say it all went away
They just want to be the superhero for a day

I'm here to tell you, you need to pick up and move
I'm here to tell you, you are not alone
Theres a feeling of being old, worn, and tired here in the zone
No future at all, here in the zone

Well, they don't care if your life crumbles and rots away
They don't care if you leave or if you stay
They just make as if they are pure and innocent
They just want to sweep you like dirt under the carpet

Thee

written 7/20/23

How many times can I count the ways
In your mind, in your heart
How many ways can I portray
How I love thee, how I want

The peaceful nights that come so rare
A place for thee to feel safe and dear
Midnight comes but once an eve
Heart shaped box for all to see
In my guts and in my soul
My grip on thee won't let thee go

Life with thee is what dreams are made of
In my rhymes, in my sonnets
Life undone can be restarted
How I hold thee, how I bonded

The winds of change blow from the
East
A place for thee to sail the seas
The morning brings calm and peace
Sunrise and hope to fill the streets
In my castle and in my chateau
My grip on thee won't let thee go

There She Blows

written 7/22/23

Stroke it and squeeze it until it unleashes
Change up the flow and watch it all go
Like paint on a canvas a true work of art
Brush up and down, stop and restart

Bring your hands in the mix with a tug and a twist
Don't be afraid to add lots of spit
Never surrender and never complain
Give it your best shot and step up your game

Hot spew, fire and ash about to unload
Like an active volcano, there she blows

Bring your sister or bring your best friend
There's plenty of room for them to attend
Say what you will say what you want
Practice makes perfect to work on your skills

Push it and shove it until it goes in
Move your hips with rhythm and motion
Face to face an eye for an eye
Honey it's too late to be acting all shy

Hot spew, fire and ash about to unload
Like an active volcano, there she blows

This Heart Of Mine

written 12/12/23

I love the flowers and I love the crazies
I pick them good like roses and daisies
I love my freedom and I love to rein
It shines like glory like the light of day

This heart of mine is the key to match
To understand and to hold and catch
This heart of mine will bleed for you
Make your dreams forever true

I love the ocean and I love the sea
It smells like rain like a summer breeze
I love my children and I love the voices
It sounds like heaven like joyful noises

This heart of mine is the key to match
To understand and to hold and catch
This heart of mine will bleed for you
Make your dreams forever true

I love the mountains and I love the trees
They grow like giants like folk tale stories
I love to make peace and I love to hug
It gives me power like a cord and plug

Tiny Kisses On My Cheek

written 1/24

She makes me feel better when I'm feeling bad
And brings me happy meals when I'm feeling sad
She lifts me up when I'm feeling down
And finds my coat from the lost and found

My world, my universe, my air to breath
She's the tiny kisses on my cheek
My flower, my queen, my honeybee
She's the tiny kisses on my cheek

She keeps me young when I'm feeling old
And lights my fire when I'm feeling cold
She runs in my dreams when I fall asleep
And blesses my heart and soul to keep

My world, my universe, my air to breath
She's the tiny kisses on my cheek
My flower, my queen, my honeybee
She's the tiny kisses on my cheek

To The Moon

written 11/20/23

The future is here, and the past is gone
The smile in my voice tells it all
My rhymes and poems go tongue and cheek
A path that circles is quite unique

From out of this world- To the oceans and seas
Follow her to the moon- And for eternity

From the center of earth- To the rivers and streams
Follow her to the moon- And everywhere in between

Her hair is short, and her nails grow long
The pied piper sings my song

She brings the heat and warms my soul
Rides with me on my journey home

From out of this world- To the oceans and seas
Follow her to the moon- And for eternity

From the center of earth- To the rivers and streams
Follow her to the moon- And everywhere in between

Bridge-
Spotlights and green eyes
Like something I never seen
Reminds me of an actress
Like a star in a movie scene

Tom The Turkey

written 11/22/23

Tom likes to play with the kids and go for long car rides
Tom likes to run, skip, and walk but he's too heavy to fly

Tom likes to rise with the chickens and wake up early
Tom doesn't know he is just a piece of turkey

Tom likes to stay up late and watch scary movies
Tom likes to be lazy and sit on his big booty

Tom likes to eat breast meat and spicy beef jerky
Tom doesn't know he is just a piece of turkey

Tom likes to impress the hens and show off his feathers
Tom likes to stuff his face with garlic wings from Hooters

Tom likes to live free and ride on his
soft tail Harley
Tom doesn't know he is just a piece
of turkey

Too Much Money

written 8/10/23

I think back to the days
Back when I couldn't get laid
I made a deal with the devil
And man did I get paid

I'm just the kid next door
With all the talent in the world
I made my way to the top
Before my mind got disturbed

I can't hear you
There's too much money in my hand
I can't see you
I'm just hanging with my fans

I'm the number one draft pick
Got my suit and hair cut slick
Now your wife is my next date
And your mom knows all my tricks

I live a rich and famous life
I like to hip and hop all night
I paid a very steep price tag
I'm not that good with your advice

I can't hear you
There's too much money in my hand
I can't see you
I'm just hanging with my fans

I think back to the nights
I played under the Friday lights
Now I'm flying on private jets
Around the world on non-stop flights

You know I don't kiss and tell
But my name Is Johnny Manzeil
I used to sleep in a penthouse
Now I'm just living in Scottsdale

Vikings Always Return

written 11/15/23

Look in the mirror- what do I see
Is it my imagination- or is it still me

Oh, my aching body- why do you
creak in the night
Oh, my aching body- Please don't
give up the fight

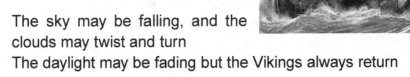

The sky may be falling, and the
clouds may twist and turn
The daylight may be fading but the Vikings always return

Look in the mirror- who can it be
Is it my father- or is it still me

Oh, my aging body- where did my time go so fast
Oh, my aging body- You're such a blast from the past

The sky may be falling, and the clouds may twist and turn
The daylight may be fading but the Vikings always return

Who Am I

written 7/30/23

I'm not a dancer but I know it takes two to Tango
I'm not a musician but I'm grand as a piano
I'm not a book but I can read between the lines
I'm not a topic of discussion but I'm always on your mind

Time to sink or swim or go off on the deep end
Time to come to terms, no regrets, no returns
Feeling sick or feeling fine, what the hell am I
Flying low or flying high, what the hell am I

I'm not as sharp as a knife but I'm on the cutting edge
I'm not suicidal but I'm standing on the ledge
I'm not unemployed but I only work part time
I'm not a needle but I'm a thread passing thru the eye

Time to sink or swim or go off on the deep end
Time to come to terms, no regrets, no returns
I can see but I am blind, what the hell am I
Flying low or flying high, what the hell am I

214

Wicked Brew

written 7/17/23

Walk right up, walk right in
Have a seat, how ya been
Hit the lights and make a scene
Feed the dragon fine cuisine

Looks great, taste smooth, lean back, drink a few
Bold, sharp, and strong, sweet- wicked brew
Looks great, taste smooth, black label, 100 proof
Rich, dark, and cold, sweet- wicked brew

Center left to center right
High bar tops and neon lights
I'm your daisy if you pick me up
Keep it chill and on the rocks

Looks great, taste smooth, lean back, drink a few
Bold, sharp, and strong, sweet- wicked brew
Looks great, taste smooth, black label, 100 proof
Rich, dark, and cold, sweet- wicked brew

Duty calls and it's getting late
Now its time to shake and bake
Feeling good, feeling great
Take me home, shoot me straight

Winter Is Coming

written 7/21/23

Blue diamond eyes, shine in the night
Hunting down your soul, sucking out your life
No one will escape, no wall will keep you safe
Only wizards and spells, will help you thru the day

Winter is coming, it will be the death of us all
Frozen tundra, ice and sleet, gusty winds, and intense squalls
Winter is coming, pure as the driven snow
It will be a white out, blizzard skies and bone chill cold

Rusty cage halos, a bright Winter glow
Still too light to see, the blackness of a crow
No one will see the end; it comes too fast to defend
The evil frost that bites you, sleep is your only friend

Winter is coming, it will be the death of us all
Frozen tundra, ice and sleet, gusty winds, and intense squalls
Winter is coming, pure as the driven snow
It will be a white out, blizzard skies and bone chill cold

Wolf In Sheep's Clothing

written 1-24

I owe the bank of England and I can't afford to lose
I'm the royal Prince of nothing but I own the house of blues
I got a ton of imagination, started lying before I could talk
I got a nasty reputation, I'm the world's greatest fraud

I'm a wolf in sheep's clothing- Howling in the night
I huff and I bluff- As I smile and I bite
I'm a wolf in sheep's clothing- Preying in the night
I run with a pack- As I hunt and I fright

I'm a product of the system, just a pawn in the game
I'm a sucker for some wisdom so I watch before I play
I'm no different than a bullfrog resting on the bank
Swallowing worms and insects, I take all that I can take

I'm a wolf in sheep's clothing-
Howling in the night
I huff and I bluff- As I smile and I bite
I'm a wolf in sheep's clothing-
Preying in the night
I run with a pack- As I hunt and I
fright

Would You Leave This World

written 12/14/23

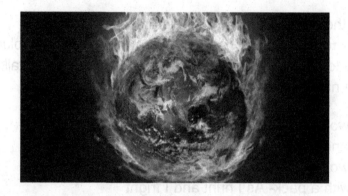

If there was no sun to shine on me
No heat, no light, no energy
If there was no moon to follow you
No waves, no night, no gravity pull

Would you still hold my hand- Would you still care
Would you still count the ways- Would you persevere

Would you leave this world behind and live life in the blind
Would you close your eyes forever or open up your mind

If there were no stars to lead the way
No signs, no glow, no violet rays
If there was no rain to fall on us
No lakes, no ponds, no water cups

Would you still wake up with me- Would you still fall asleep
Would you still make your bed- Would you take the leap

Would you leave this world behind and live life in the blind
Would you close your eyes forever or open up your mind

You'll Be The Death Of Me

written 11/29/23

Looking fine in your evening dress
You got it right off the hot press
I know you like to stay out all night
But where ya been gets me all uptight

Running wild and running free
Honey child- you'll be the death of me
Barley legal at age 18
Honey child, you'll be the death of me

Make believe what you cannot see
You can bring the devil to his knees
I know you want to be all grown up
Fly the coop and take the jump

Running wild and running free
Honey child- you'll be the death of me
Barley legal at age 18
Honey child, you'll be the death of me

Printed in the United States
by Baker & Taylor Publisher Services

Printed in the United States
by Baker & Taylor Publisher Services